THREE CENTURIES OF NURSERY RHYMES AND POETRY FOR CHILDREN

A

Books on Child Life and Literature
by Iona and Peter Opie, published by
Oxford :

The Oxford Dictionary of Nursery Rhymes

The Oxford Nursery Rhyme Book

The Lore and Language of Schoolchildren

Children's Games in Street & Playground

The Oxford Book of Children's Verse

THREE CENTURIES

OF

NURSERY RHYMES

AND

POETRY FOR CHILDREN

An Exhibition held at
The National Book League
May 1973

Presented by
IONA (archibald) & PETER OPIE

Oxford University Press Ely House London W 1

GLASGOW NEW YORK TORONTO MELBOURNE WELLINGTON
CAPE TOWN IBADAN NAIROBI DAR ES SALAAM LUSAKA ADDIS ABABA
DELHI BOMBAY CALCUTTA MADRAS KARACHI LAHORE DACCA
KUALA LUMPUR SINGAPORE HONG KONG TOKYO

ISBN 019 211554 5

Printed in Great Britain

Introduction   5

Nursery Rhymes

1 First Sightings   9
2 Classic Collections   11
3 Popular and Period Collections   16
4 Illustrious Illustrators   27

    J. C. Horsley and others
    Thomas Webster
    John Absolon, Harrison Weir, and others
    E. V. Boyle
    Charles H. Bennett
    H. S. Marks
    John Millais
    Keeley Halswelle
    Alfred Crowquill
    Marcus Ward
    Walter Crane
    Randolph Caldecott
    Kate Greenaway
    Alice B. Woodward
    Paul Woodroffe
    L. Leslie Brooke
    Cecil Aldin
    Byam Shaw
    John Hassall
    H. Willebeek Le Mair
    Arthur Rackham
    Claud Lovat Fraser
    Lawson Wood
    Charles Folkard
    Mervyn Peake
    Alexander Calder
    Joan Hassall
    Maurice Sendak
    Charles Addams

5 Celebrated Characters   32

    Cock Robin and Jenny Wren
    Dame Trot

    Dish that Ran Away with the Spoon
    Hungry Fox
    Frogs, Waddling and Wooing
    Humpty Dumpty
    Jack the House Builder
    Jack and Jill
    Jack Horner
    Jack Jingle
    Jack Sprat
    Jacky Dandy
    Jumping Joan
    Kings and Queens
    Little Kittens
    Men and Maids
    Blind Mice
    Miller of Dee
    Mother Goose
    Mother Hubbard
    Peter Piper
    Little Pigs
    Simple Simon
    Tom the Piper's Son
    Tommy Tucker
    Little Market Woman
    Old Woman who Bought a Pig
    Old Woman who Lived in a Shoe
    Old Woman Tossed in a Basket
    Yankee Doodle
    Duke of York

6 Two Alphabets   48
    A was an Apple Pie
    A was an Archer

7 Histories and Interpretations   50
8 Transformations and Translations   53
9 Nursery Rhymes in Advertising   56
10 Nursery Rhyme Novelties   58

Poetry for Children

First and Early Appearances of
Well-known Poems   59

Introduction

*'He who pleases the children will be remembered
with pleasure by the men'*

JAMES BOSWELL

This exhibition consists, as its name gives warning, of books for the young, and the very young. It contains books in which some of our best-known verses for children first appeared: 'The Pobble who has no toes', 'There are fairies at the bottom of our garden', and

'January brings the snow,
Makes our feet and fingers glow;'

and it contains books in which the most familiar of our traditional rhymes are first found, rhymes such as 'The House that Jack built', 'Little Boy Blue come blow your horn', and 'Boys and girls come out to play'. Indeed, we have here, very certainly, a greater assortment of nursery rhyme and nonsense books than it has hitherto been felt prudent to expose in one place at one time; and we are conscious that if this light-hearted assemblage is to be considered of anything more than infant interest we must produce more substantial justification than that the rhymes contained in these books are the most renowned compositions in the English language.

We might suggest, for instance, that the sight of the same corpus of old verses being reprinted over and over again by one generation of publishers after another was wonderful testimony to the economy of human invention; or that the pictorial representation of these rhymes, in which the illustrations tell us more about the times in which they were executed than about the subjects being depicted, demonstrate man's unswerving propensity for viewing the past in terms of the present. (Notice, by the way, how Mother Hubbard, who first appeared as a Regency crone, is updated during the next hundred years, until she becomes an Edwardian matron.) We might even remark how pictures of coffins and tipsy old women are no longer the fashion in modern nursery rhyme books, and how even references to cats catching mice, and other such ascertainable facts of life, are now liable to be censored, revealing, it appears, an undercurrent of squeamishness and prudery in an age deemed violent and permissive.

Perhaps, however, we should content ourselves with the suggestion that we are displaying here some of the most delightful books ever published, as also some of the world's rarest; and make the point that it is no coincidence when these two attributes are found in one and the same volume. Dull books, like dull politicians, survive by the very fact that they are dull: they remain in good condition through our unwillingness to become involved with them. The majority of old books that occupy the shelves of antiquarian booksellers today are no more typical of the popular reading of their day than are the numerous worthy but unreadable volumes of our own time. The books that were most read in the past, and in particular the children's books that were most read in the past, were literally read to pieces. Indeed, it is an axiom, or if it isn't it should be, that the books which are most scarce today are the books which gave most pleasure in their own day; and in this exhibition we can point, as evidence, to such a lovely item as the first magazine for children, *The Lilliputian Magazine*, 1752, of which only one other copy is known; or to the enlarged edition of *Little Goody Two-Shoes*, 1766, which is likewise one of two recorded copies—the other being in America; or to the first edition of Christopher Smart's *Hymns for Children*, 1771, here making its public *début*; or to that notorious rarity of the nineteenth century, Lear's *Book of Nonsense*, 1846, both parts in their original pictorial card covers, as also to the joyous and infinitely scarce book of limerick-style verses, *Anecdotes and Adventures of Fifteen Gentlemen*, which preceded Lear by more than twenty years; and from which he had the idea for his own 'nonsenses'.

Other books on show, delightful but of later date, may still be procurable; but are by no means common if required—as they should be—in pristine condition. Books that are rebound or worn or torn or dirty can, in our view, do almost a disservice in the message they bring from the past. They make former times appear tired. We look at a long-loved relic and are scarcely able to imagine it was once a shining novelty. So we have made it our care to show books that are, as near as possible, in their original state, though admitting there are instances where we are still seeking finer copies.

This seems the more worthwhile when it is remembered that nursery rhymes have been so constant an ingredient of children's literature that they have been published in almost every shape and style of book that has been manufactured; and that we can trace in the exhibits here virtually the whole history of book production for the young. Indeed, the very first books produced for children, that is to say the first produced genuinely for children's amusement rather than instruction, were nursery rhyme books; and we are able to show a dainty eighteenth-century American edition of the little book believed to be the actual starting-point, early in 1744, of the age of levity: the long unidentified volume I of *Tommy Thumb's Pretty Song Book*.

In fact, by arranging the books as much as possible chronologically (rather than categorising them, as has been felt most useful in this catalogue), and by displaying a concourse of cheap editions side by side: shilling books, sixpenny books, and penny books—most of all penny books (and halfpenny books too), the little coverless 'chapbooks' printed for distribution by pedlars or chapmen who trudged the country roads, offering them at cottage doors as they journeyed between fairs and market places—by displaying a full wall of these publications, all of them related to the same subject and thus directly comparable, we are able to present a panorama of popular printing over the past two hundred years, and show, as in no other way, the technical changes that have taken place since the days of a rural economy.

Thus we can see the crude woodcuts of the eighteenth century refined under the influence of Bewick, so that to a layman (such as George III) they became almost indistinguishable from copperplates; we can admire the early nineteenth-century copperplates enriched by professional hand-colourists (themselves often children); can examine the woodblock printing with oil colours which in its early days bore a remarkable resemblance to hand-colouring (compare *The History of A, Apple Pie*, produced by Dean & Son in 1851, with *A was an Archer* published by Dean probably at Christmas 1867); and can follow, as the century grows older, the elaboration of the colour designs on the covers of the toy-books, as well as within.

6

Indeed, since the literary content of nursery rhyme books has remained constant, the higher class publishers in the second half of the nineteenth century (many of them, such as Dean, Macmillan, Routledge, Warne, and Ward Lock, still in business today) used every method they could contrive to make their books more desirable than those of their rivals. They engaged the most able illustrators of the day: Crowquill, Charles Bennett, H. S. Marks, Marcus Ward, Harrison Weir, Walter Crane, Randolph Caldecott, and Kate Greenaway. They printed the books on boards, or linen-backed paper, or on 'rag', so that their productions could be described as 'indestructible' or 'waterproof' or 'washable'. They made 'magic' nursery rhyme books, 'surprise' nursery rhyme books, 'movable' nursery rhyme books, 'scenic' nursery rhyme books, and, in the twentieth century, singing nursery rhyme books—books which could be played on a gramophone. They made nursery rhyme panoramas (one here is over 7 feet long), and shaped books, and painting books; and in the twentieth century, transfer books, and cut-out model books, and post-card books. They have made topical books, in which the nursery rhyme characters ride bicycles, or fight battles, or, following Alice, inhabit versions of Wonderland. They have even made believe one nursery rhyme book was dug up from the pyramids, wrapped in Mummy cloth. Almost the only thing they have not done for nursery rhymes is take trouble with the texts, for that—as we know, and perhaps as they knew—requires perseverance and patience, virtues that seldom bring an economic return.

The section of books containing poetry specially written for children completes the publishing story because here, indisputably, the texts are significant. Some of the books in which well-known poems first appeared, such as Ann and Jane Taylor's *Original Poems, for Infant Minds*, 1804 (which included 'My Mother'), Mrs Alexander's *Hymns for Little Children*, 1848 (containing 'All things bright and beautiful'), and even Stevenson's *A Child's Garden of Verses*, 1885, were in their original editions modest little volumes that, judged by appearance, one would not bother to pick out at a 5p. charity bookstall. They possess but a single picture between them; and aesthetically may well have been the better for it, since the majority of pictures that accompany poetry tend to confine the imagination rather than release it. In fact these little books are a reminder, if ever we need reminding, that glorious as is the product of the visual arts, the images that live with us most intimately, in childhood as in maturity, are those that come to us through the printed word.

For mounting this exhibition we are deeply grateful to the Oxford University Press, and in particular to Miss Elizabeth Knight whose enthusiasm has been unflagging, and to other members of the Press who have helped us; as also to Mr Kenneth Breese and Mr Alan Breese for designing the exhibition; and to the National Book League for playing host, and having a staff willing to give us such powerful assistance. We are also grateful to our sons, James and Robert, for practical support, as in all things, from the outset; and to Mr Nicolas Barker of the Oxford University Press for designing this catalogue and over-seeing its production.

Every compiler of a catalogue cherishes the hope that, no matter how short-lived his exhibition, the record of it will be of lasting interest, and we give assurance we are no different in this respect from our fellows. We have felt this catalogue would be most useful if planned as an adjunct to *The Oxford Dictionary of Nursery Rhymes* and *The Oxford Book of Children's Verse*, hoping it will serve almost as a bibliography for anyone wishing to make further study of English traditional verse, or poetry for children, or perhaps even childrens' book production. We have thus made it our object to give details that do not appear in our other works. In particular we have transcribed the title and full imprint of virtually every one of the books appearing here: the imprints being essential, when books are undated, if one printing is to be distinguished from another, and sometimes if one publication is to be distinguished from another. We have also done our best to determine the dates; though aware of how much work still needs to be done, particularly on the chapbooks and toybooks of the middle years of the nineteenth century.

Perhaps, too, this catalogue will have interest as the first notice of a particular collection. The books and ephemera described here are a section, or more accurately cross-section, of the material we have been assembling over many years to document and illustrate Child Life and Literature. Such a gathering of material, if it is also to be useful to its custodians, can only be maintained in a personal way. It is impracticable, as others have found, to be both a public curator and a productive research-worker. Yet anyone building up what will one day, presumably, be a public archive, is liable on occasion to question his aims and examine his philosophy. He wishes to know whether what he is doing is thought worth doing, and whether the way he is doing it is the best way. Every exhibition, and this one is no exception, is a kind of manifesto. If these treasures from the recesses of nursery cupboards are found to be even half as delightful, and as historically revealing, as we feel they are, we shall be more than gratified.

I. &. P.O.

1 First Sightings

Many nursery rhymes are known to have been in existence long before there were nursery rhyme books. Stray references to them have been found in various types of literature of the sixteenth, seventeenth, and eighteenth centuries: in plays, satires, dictionaries, adult song books, and even in religious books. In this section we show the actual places where some familiar rhymes have first been sighted. And to show that research in adult literature can be profitable even in the period when nursery rhyme books had become common, we include three well-known rhymes that, perhaps surprisingly, are not found until the nineteenth century.

1 QVEEN ANNA'S NEW WORLD OF WORDS, or Dictionarie of the Italian and English tongues, Collected, and newly much augmented by Iohn Florio . . . *London, Printed by Melch. Bradwood, for Edw. Blount and William Barret.* Anno 1611.

On p. 3 *Abómba* is defined as 'properly the place, where children playing hide themselues, as at a play called king by your leaue . . . It is also a mans home or dwelling. Also as we vse to say Home againe home againe, market is done.'

ODNR no. 339. For 'king by your leaue' see *Children's Games in Street and Playground*, p. 155.

2 CAROLINE COMMONPLACE BOOK, in which, amongst hymns, Latin quotations, and recipes, one of a succession of owners has written, about 1665, possibly the earliest version of the 'Wonder of Wonders', beginning:

I saw a peacock, with a flaming tail
I saw a star, that dropt down Hail.

ODNR, no. 398.

3 A COLLECTION OF ENGLISH PROVERBS Digested into a convenient Method for the speedy finding any one upon occasion; with Short Annotations . . . By J. R. [John Ray] M.A. and Fellow of the Royal Society. *Cambridge, Printed by John Hayes, Printer to the University, for W. Morden.* 1670.

On p. 211 appears the earliest recording of the rhyme 'Jack Sprat' in the form known today. Other 'Proverbial Rhythmes' on the same page include 'Bouce buckram, velvet's dear', and 'A man of words and not of deeds'.

ODNR, nos. 264, 81, 322.

Abbreviations:
ODNR The Oxford Dictionary of Nursery Rhymes
ONRB The Oxford Nursery Rhyme Book

4 SOME OBSERVATIONS upon the Answer to An Enquiry into the Grounds and Occasions of the Contempt of the Clergy: With some Additions. In a Second Letter to R. L. By the same Author. *London, Printed for N. Brooke at the Angel in Cornhill near the Royal-Exchange.* 1671.

On p. 140 John Eachard ridicules preachers who find meaning in every letter of a word, and would exhort their congregation to repent letter by letter: 'Repent, R. readily; Repent, E. earnestly; Repent, P. presently; Repent, E. effectually; Repent, N. nationally; Repent, T. throughly . . . And also, why not,' he continues, 'A apple-pasty, B bak'd it, C cut it, D divided it, E eat it, F fought for it, G got it, &c.' If the learned divine had not chanced to use this analogy it might have been thought this famous alphabet dated only from the eighteenth century.

5 THE MUSICAL COMPANION, In Two Books. The First Book containing Catches and Rounds for Three Voyces. The Second Book containing Dialogues, Glees, Ayres and Songs for Two, Three and Four Voyces. Collected and Published by John Playford Practitioner in Musick. *London, Printed by W. Godbid for John Playford, at his Shop in the Temple near the Church,* 1673.

On p. 13 appears 'There were three Cooks of Colebrook'. This is not the first printing, but it does show the round as it originally appeared; and anyone wishing to see why some lines were not included in *ODNR* can here be satisfied.

6 THE CAMPAIGNERS: or, The Pleasant Adventures at Brussels. A Comedy As it is Acted at the Theatre Royal . . . Written by Mr. D'urfey. *London, Printed for A. Baldwin, near the Oxford Arms Inn in Warwick Lane.* 1698.

On p. 19 appears the earliest known reference to 'Pat-a-cake, pat-a-cake, baker's man'. Also on this page is part of the mock lullaby 'My dear Cockadoodle, my Jewel, my Joy.'

ODNR, no. 396.

7 USEFUL TRANSACTIONS IN PHILOSOPHY, And other sorts of Learning, For the Months of January and February, 1708/9. To be continu'd Monthly, as they Sell. *London: Printed for Bernard Lintott, at the Cross-Keys, between the two Temple-Gates, in Fleetstreet.*

On p. 44-5 of this skit, written by William King, 'Boys and girls come out to play' makes its first appearance. It is, said Dr. King, 'an English Ode, very ancient, harmonious and useful to the Publick, encouraging Youth to Exercise and Hardship'. A few pages further on he discusses with equal verve two further rhymes which no one but he had thought of putting in print: 'Good King Cole' and 'The Lyon and the Unicorn fighting for the Crown'. The doctor can scarcely have imagined the way in which his *Transactions* would be 'useful' to future generations.

8 A LEARNED DISSERTATION ON DUMPLING; Its Dignity, Antiquity, and Excellence. With a Word upon Pudding . . . The Fourth Edition. *London, Printed for J. Roberts in the Oxford-Arms Passage, Warwick-Lane; And Sold by Mrs. Nutt under the Royal Exchange, and Mrs. Dodd without Temple-Bar.* 1726. Priced 6d.

At the end appears Henry Carey's *Namby Pamby: or, A Panegyric on the New Versification*, first published the previous year, a burlesque of the verses which Ambrose Philips was writing, ostensibly addressed to children. In the burlesque Carey makes reference to eleven nursery rhymes, amongst them

Jacky Horner
Sitting in the Chimney-corner,
Eating of a Christmas-Pie,
Putting in his Thumb, Oh fie!

which had hitherto been unknown to literature.

9 LOVE IN A VILLAGE; A Comic Opera. As it is performed at the Theatre Royal in Covent-Garden. *London: Printed by W. Griffin; For J. Newbery, and W. Nicoll, in St. Paul's Church-Yard* [and others]. 1763.

In Act I, scene V, of Bickerstaffe's entertainment, John Beard in the part of Hawthorn made popular the song 'There was a jolly miller once, Liv'd on the river Dee'.

10 [NURSE TRUELOVE'S NEW YEAR'S GIFT; or, The Book of Books for Children. Adorned with cuts, and designed for a present to every little boy who would become a great man, and ride upon a fine horse, and to every little girl who would become a great woman, and ride in a Lord Mayor's gilt coach. *London: Printed for J. Newbery,*

at the Bible and Sun, in St. Paul's Church-Yard.] [1765 ?]

Unfortunately only a part remains of this minute paper-covered two-penny children's book; but no complete copy is known to exist as early as this (the date is deduced from advertisement pages), and happily pp. 31-40 are complete, giving us the earliest known printing and pictures of 'The House that Jack built'. Gift of Miss Nancy Green.

11 A NEW RIDDLE BOOK, or A Whetstone for Dull Wits. *Printed at Derby, for the Benefit of the Travelling Stationers.* [c. 1765]

On p. 9 of this chapbook, which consists for the most part of riddles whose wit lies in *double entendre*, is the excellent riddle-rhyme about a pair of shoes. 'Two brothers we are, great burthens we bear'. (*ODNR* no. 79.) This copy is possibly a reissue, c. 1790.

12 THE SCOTS MUSICAL MUSEUM. Humbly Dedicated to The Catch Club Instituted at Edinr. June 1771. By James Johnson. Vol. V. *Edinr. Printed & Sold by Johnson & Co. Music Sellers head of Lady Stair's Close, Lawn Market, where may be had variety of Music, & Musical Instruments, Instruments Lent out, Tun'd & Repair'd.* [1797]

Old King Cole made his first appearance in William King's *Useful Transactions* (see above no. 7). Shown here, on pp. 486-7, is the rollicking version Burns collected together with the tune to which it was then sung.

13 MONTHLY LITERARY RECREATIONS; or, Magazine of General Information and Amusement . . . Vol. I. For July to December, 1806. *London: Printed for B. Crosby and Co. Stationers'-Court, By Dewick and Clarke, Aldersgate-street.* 1807.

In the second number, pp. 113-7, appears a facetious essay entitled 'Critical Comments on the Bo-peepeid, an Epic-pastoral poem, in three parts' which gives for the first time (as far as is known) the text of 'Little Bo-peep'. This 'first sighting' has not hitherto been recorded.

14 TRADITIONS, LEGENDS, SUPERSTITIONS, AND SKETCHES OF DEVONSHIRE on the Borders of the Tamar and the Tavy . . . In a Series of Letters to Robert Southey, Esq. By Mrs Bray . . . In Three Volumes. Vol. II. *London: John Murray, Albemarle Street.* 1838.

On p. 287 Mrs Bray records that in Tavistock the

fortunes of children were considered 'to be very much regulated by the day on which they were born'; and she writes down, apparently before anyone else had done so, the rhyme: 'Monday's child is fair in face' (*ODNR* no. 353).

15 PUNCH. Vol. LXVIII. *London: Published at the Office, 85, Fleet Street.* 1875.

In the number for 10 April, p. 155, amongst 'Nursery Rhymes New Set for the Times' appear the now-famous lines:

> There was an owl liv'd in an oak,
> The more he heard, the less he spoke,
> The less he spoke, the more he heard—
> O, if men were all like that wise bird.

The illustration, portraying the owl as Punch, is by Linley Sambourne.

2 Classic Collections

By 'classic collections' we mean the collections which will always be valued for their antiquity, or for the quality or quantity of their texts, or for their recordings of tunes. Here are some of the books of the pioneer collectors and publishers, the collections containing rhymes not hitherto printed, the collections with the most rhymes, or the most unusual rhymes, or with the best versions: the collections made by the few people, the very few people, who have cared enough about the rhymes to gather them or regather them for themselves.

16 TOMMY THUMB'S SONG BOOK, for all little Masters and Misses. To be Sung to them by their Nurses, until they can sing themselves. By Nurse Lovechild. To which is added, A Letter from a Lady on Nursing. The Second Worcester Edition. *Printed at Worcester, Massachusetts, by Isaiah Thomas, Sold Wholesale and Retail at his Bookstore.* 1794.

This is believed to be an edition of the first ⌐nursery rhyme book, published in 1744, the contents of which have long been the subject of conjecture. It is generally accepted that the earliest known nursery rhyme book is *Tommy Thumb's Pretty Song Book,* of which the only surviving copy is in the British Museum, and is styled 'Voll II'. An advertisement for it, first discovered by Miss Margaret Weedon, appeared in *The London Evening Post,* 19–22 May 1744. However, two months earlier, in the number for 17–22 March, the same publisher announced: 'This Day is publish'd, Price 6d. bound, Tommy Thumb's Song Book for all little Masters and Misses; to be sung to them by their Nurses 'till they can sing them themselves. By Nurse Lovechild. To which is added, a Letter from a Lady on Nursing.' This, it will be seen, is precisely the title of the little book Isaiah Thomas printed in Worcester; and since it was Thomas's practice to reprint children's books published in London virtually without alteration (he first printed this title in 1788), and since no advertisement has been found of a *Tommy Thumb's PRETTY Song Book,* vol. I, it is reasonable to assume that we have in this volume the contents of the lost volume I, that is to say of the first nursery rhyme book. The copy is in its original blue-green Dutch paper covers. Welch no. 737. Only one copy recorded of this edition.

17 TOMMY THUMB'S SONG-BOOK . . . *Glasgow: Published by J. Lumsden & Son.* 1815.

A Scottish abridgement printed seventy-one years after this title was first advertised.

18 THE FAMOUS TOMMY THUMB'S LITTLE STORY-BOOK: containing His Life and surprising Adventures. To which are added, Tommy Thumb's Fables, with Morals: and at the End, pretty Stories, that may be either sung or told. Adorned with many curious Pictures. *London: Printed for S. Crowder, in Pater-Noster-Row; and sold by B. Collins, at the Printing-Office, in Salisbury, and by most eminent Booksellers.* [c. 1760]

The 'pretty stories, that may be either sung or told' are nine nursery rhymes ('Little Boy Blue' and 'This pig went to market' amongst them), and their inclusion along with fables in this miniature miscellany confirms that two hundred years ago nursery rhymes were already recognised as being part of the staple literature of the young. This is, in fact, one of the three earliest known collections of nursery rhymes, and the first to have also (in 1768) been published in America.

19 MOTHER GOOSE'S MELODY: or, Sonnets for the Cradle. In Two Parts. Part I. Contains the most celebrated Songs and Lullabies of the old

British Nurses, calculated to amuse Children and to excite them to sleep. . . . Embellished with Cuts. And illustrated with Notes and Maxims, Historical, Philosophical and Critical. *London: Printed for Francis Power (Grandson to the late Mr. J. Newbery), and Co. No. 65. St. Paul's Church Yard, 1791.*

Facsimile of the earliest known copy (now in the Pierpont Morgan Library) of the most influential of early collections. The book was entered at Stationers' Hall, 28 December 1780; but it may have been compiled some years earlier, and a not improbable tradition associates Oliver Goldsmith with its editorship. *ODNR* pp. 34–35 and plate IX.

20 MOTHER GOOSE'S MELODY: or Sonnets for the Cradle. . . . The Second Worcester Edition. *Worcester, (Massachusetts). Printed by Isaiah Thomas, and sold at his Bookstore. 1794.*

Facsimile of the earliest surviving American edition.

21 MOTHER GOOSE'S MELODY: or, Sonnets for the Cradle: containing the most celebrated Songs and Lullabies of the Old British Nurses. Embellished with many Beautiful Pictures. *London: Printed and Sold by John Marshall, 140, Fleet Street, From Aldermary Church-Yard. 1816*

A well-loved copy of a late edition. All editions are scarce (none appears to be known by more than a single copy), which in itself is evidence of their popularity. Other than the frontispiece (reproduced in *ODNR* plate VIII), the illustrations are the same as those appearing in eighteenth century editions, and have been hand-coloured to keep up with the times.

22 READING MADE QUITE EASY AND DIVERTING. Containing Symbolical Cuts for the Alphabet; Tables of Words of one, two, three and four Syllables, with easy Lessons from the Scriptures, at the End of each Table . . . instructive Fables and edifying Pieces of Poetry, with Songs, moral and divine, from I. Watts. . . . With several entertaining Stories, Proverbs, moral Sayings, Riddles, &c., and curious alphabetical Gimcracks. A New Edition, new modelled, greatly enlarged and improved. By Tom Thumb, a Lover of Children, W. Wield, and others. *London: Printed, and sold by all the Booksellers, 1789.*

Contains a group of twelve nursery rhymes entitled 'Pretty little Songs and Stories for young Masters and Misses', and six under other headings.

23 A CHOICE COLLECTION OF RIDDLES, Charades, Rebusses, &c. Chiefly Original.

By Peter Puzzlewell, Esq. *London: Printed for E. Newbery, Corner of St. Paul's Church-yard. 1794*

Contains a number of traditional riddle rhymes; and also some catches such as 'King Charles walk'd and talk'd, seven years after his head was cut off'.

24 [BAPTIST NOEL TURNER] Infant Institutes, Part the First. Or, a Nurserical Eassy on the Poetry, Lyric and Allegorical of the Earlier Ages. With an Appendix. *London: Printed for and sold by F. and C. Rivingtons, St. Paul's Church-Yard. 1797*

A not very elevated essay, except where the prodigious footnotes push it to the page-top; but a work, nevertheless, that introduces the texts of twenty-two nursery rhymes. In the tradition of Mother Goose literature the pamphlet is extraordinarily scarce. No other copy has been located. *ODNR* p. 36.

25 A CHRISTMAS BOX Containing the following Bagatelles Goosy Goosy Gander, See Saw Margery Daw, Little Jack Horner, Sat in a Corner [and nine others]. Set to Music by Mr. Hook. *London: Printed & Sold at A. Bland & Weller's Music Warehouse, 23 Oxford Street.* [1797]

Piano or harp accompaniments by James Hook, the father of Theodore Hook.

26 SECOND VOLUME OF CHRISTMAS BOX. Containing the Following Bagatelles For Juvenile Amusement High ding a ding, Christmas comes but once a Yr., Little Tom Tucker [and nine others]. Set to Music by Mr. Hook. *London: Printed & Sold at A. Bland & Weller's Music Warehouse, No. 23 Oxford Street. Also by G. Walker, 106 Gt. Portland Street, and 64 Burlington Arcade.* [1798]

27 HOOK'S ORIGINAL CHRISTMAS BOX, Vol. III. Containing the Following Bagatelles For Juvenile Amusement. When Cockle Shells turn silver bells, Ba Ba Black Sheep, Taffy was a Welchman [and nine others]. Composed and Dedicated to Miss Colombine, by James Hook. *London: Printed & Sold at Bland & Wellers Music Warehouse, No. 23 Oxford Street, also by G. Walker, 106, Gt. Portland Street & 64, Burlington Arcade.* [1798]

28 THE NEW CHRISTMAS BOX, Containing a Variety of Bagatelles, Arranged For One, two, or three Voices, and the Piano Forte, for Juvenile Amusement. *London: Printed & Sold by Preston & Son, at their Wholesale Warehouses 97 Strand.* [c. 1798]

Contains twelve songs.

29 THE FAIRING, A Collection of Juvenile Songs, Adapted For One, Two, or Three Voices; With an Accompaniment for the Piano-Forte. *London: Printed & Sold by Preston & Son at their Wholesale Warehouses 97 Strand.* [c. 1799]

A successor to *The New Christmas Box* containing twelve more songs.

30 GAMMER GURTON'S GARLAND: or, the Nursery Parnassus. A Choice Collection of Pretty Songs and Verses, for the Amusement of all Little Good Children who can neither Read nor Run. *London: Printed for R. Triphook, 37, St. James's Street; By Harding and Wright, St. John's-square.* 1810.

A collection of 134 rhymes divided into four parts. The editor of the first two parts, which were published in 1784, was the literary antiquarian Joseph Ritson. Parts III and IV, here first published, contain many additional rhymes, collected by Francis Douce and others. The book is open at the earliest known printing of Humpty Dumpty. *ODNR*, pp. 35–36.

31 DAME DEARLOVE'S DITTIES FOR THE NURSERY; so wonderfully contrived, that they may be either Sung or Said by Nurse or Baby. *London: Printed for J. Harris and Son, Corner of St. Paul's Church-yard.* 1820.

No. 7 in Harris's Cabinet of Amusement and Instruction. This is an illustrated partial reprint, first produced in 1819, of *Original Ditties for the Nursery.* See below.

32 DITTIES FOR THE NURSERY 'So wonderfully contrived that they may be either sung or said, by Nurse or Baby.' Edited by Iona Opie. Illustrated by Monica Walker. *Geoffrey Cumberlege, Oxford University Press.* 1954.

An edition of *Original Ditties for the Nursery,* first published by John Harris c. 1805, and subsequently abridged as *Dame Dearlove's Ditties for the Nursery* (see above), which contains several rhymes, such as 'Little Jenny Flinders', that are now traditional.

33 SONGS FOR THE NURSERY, Collected from the Works of the Most Renowned Poets, and adapted to Favourite National Melodies. *London: Printed for William Darton, 58, Holborn Hill.* 1822.

First published in 1805 without illustrations; the fine plates (the first full-page illustrations of nursery rhymes) were added in 1818. *ODNR*, pp. 36–37 and plate XII.

34 SONGS FOR THE NURSERY. A New Edition, with Copious Additions. *London: Darton and Clark, Holborn Hill.* [c. 1845]

This enlarged edition even contains part of 'The Cataract of Lodore' (*Oxford Book of Children's Verse*, no. 93).

35 SONGS FOR THE NURSERY. *Darton & Co. London.* [First and Second Series, 1856? and 1859?]

Although having the same title and issued by the same publishing house, the contents have only a coincidental similarity with the previous collection.

36 LITTLE RHYMES, FOR LITTLE FOLKS. By a Lady, Author of "Cato," "Infant's Friend," Etc. *London: John Harris, St. Paul's Church-yard.* [c. 1824]

One of 'Harris's Cabinet of Amusement and Instruction'. Described on the cover as a new edition, and given the sub-title 'Poetry for Fanny's Library'. Most of the rhymes are decidedly lame, but three have made the journey to the present day: *ODNR* nos. 46, 106, and 532.

37 ROBERT CHAMBERS. The Popular Rhymes of Scotland, with Illustrations, Chiefly Collected from Oral Sources. *Edinburgh: William Hunter, 23, Hanover Street, Charles Smith & Co. 25, Hanover Street, and James Duncan, London.* 1826.

At the end of the book are 'Specimens of Unpublished Classes of Popular Rhymes', of which the third class is 'Nursery Rhymes'. The section contains four rhymes only, and their fewness today seems curious. But this was nevertheless a pioneer appeal to Scotsmen to 'crack credit with their grandmothers, by inquiring after such homely and foolish things'.

38 [ROBERT CHAMBERS] Popular Rhymes, Fireside Stories, and Amusements, of Scotland. Collected by the Author of "Traditions of Edinburgh". *Edinburgh: Published by William and Robert Chambers.* 1842

The success of Chambers' appeal in 1826 may be judged from the fact that he here records more than fifty rhymes and songs for the nursery, many of them of considerable interest.

39 ROBERT CHAMBERS. Popular Rhymes of Scotland. New Edition. *W. & R. Chambers. London and Edinburgh.* 1870

In this edition (the fourth) the nursery rhymes are given pride of place at the beginning of the volume; and many further rhymes, now considered nursery property, appear elsewhere in the book. In fact this work has been drawn upon by the nursery anthologists, usually without acknowledgement, unceasingly ever since.

40 MOTHER GOOSE'S MELODIES. The only Pure Edition. Containing all that have ever come to light of her Memorable Writings, together with those which have been discovered among the MSS. of Herculaneum . . . The Whole Compared, Revised, and Sanctioned, by one of The Annotators of the Goose Family. With Many New Engravings. Entered, according to Act of Congress, in the year 1833, by Munroe & Francis . . . *New York and Boston: C. S. Francis and Company.*

An excellent facsimile of an edition of about 1842 of the most influential of nursery rhyme collections to originate in America. Produced in 1970 by Dover Publications, Inc., with excellent bibliographical notes by E. F. Bleiler. The gift of the editor.

41 JAMES ORCHARD HALLIWELL. The Nursery Rhymes of England, Collected principally from Oral Tradition. *London: Printed for the Percy Society, by T. Richards, for the Executors of the late C. Richards, 100, St. Martin's Lane.* 1842

First edition of the collection which, with its historical annotation, was to form the basis of almost every nursery rhyme book of note for the next hundred years. Halliwell's virtue was that he collected as an antiquarian rather than as a commercial editor looking for an attractive subject. Nevertheless scarcely any of the rhymes—if any at all—were orally collected. Two of Halliwell's sources were nos. 30 and 33.

42 JAMES ORCHARD HALLIWELL. The Nursery Rhymes of England . . . Second Edition, with alterations and additions. *London: John Russell Smith, 4 Old Compton Street, Soho Square.* 1843

This edition, the first to be produced commercially, contains 410 numbered rhymes, against 300 in the previous edition.

43 JAMES ORCHARD HALLIWELL. The Nursery Rhymes of England . . . Third Edition, with Illustrations. *London: John Russell Smith,* 1844

Contains 468 rhymes. The illustrations are by W. B. Scott.

44 JAMES ORCHARD HALLIWELL. The Nursery Rhymes of England . . . Fourth Edition, with Illustrations. *London: John Russell Smith.* 1846

This is the third edition, with a supplement, paged 205–236, inserted between pp. 204 and 205. Contains 547 rhymes.

45 JAMES ORCHARD HALLIWELL. The Nursery Rhymes of England . . . The Sixth Edition. *London: John Russell Smith.* [c. 1855]

A reprint of the fifth edition, the Preface of which is dated 1853. Contains 659 rhymes.

46 JAMES ORCHARD HALLIWELL. Nursery Rhymes and Nursery Tales of England. With illustrations. *London: Frederick Warne and Co. Bedford Street, Strand. New York: Scribner, Welford, and Armstrong.* [c. 1868]

After 1853 Halliwell did not enlarge or amend his collection, despite several requests; but this edition does contain some additional footnotes. The illustrations are by several hands. See also no. 625.

47 JAMES ORCHARD HALLIWELL. The Nursery Rhymes of England . . . With Illustrations by W. B. Scott. *London and New York: Frederick Warne and Co.* 1886.

A large-paper reprint of the Fifth Edition.

48 E. F. RIMBAULT. Nursery Rhymes, with the Tunes to which they are Still Sung in the Nurseries of England. Obtained Principally from Oral Tradition. Collected and Edited by Edward F. Rimbault, LL.D, F.S.A., &c. &c. *London: Cramer, Beale, & Co., 201, Regent Street, and 67, Conduit Street.* [1846]

Many times reprinted, the collection is of value for the tunes rather than the texts. The preface is almost wholly taken from Halliwell, a fact which did not cement their friendship.

49 [E. F. RIMBAULT] A Collection of Old Nursery Rhymes, With Familiar Tunes for Voice and Pianoforte. Adapted to the Capacities of Young Folk. *London: Chappell and Co., 50 New Bond Street.* [1864]

Revised edition, published eighteen years later, and offered as being 'perhaps more suited to the present generation of young folk.'

50 M. H. MASON. Nursery Rhymes and Country Songs, Both Tunes and Words from Tradition. With Illustrations by Miss E. M. S. Scannell. Collected and Arranged by M. H. Mason. *London: Metzler & Co. 37 Great Marlborough Street.* [1878]

One of the earliest collections of songs and tunes gathered from oral tradition, the compiler having learned many of them from her Northumbrian grandmother. A second edition, with a few additions, was published in 1909.

51 SABINE BARING-GOULD. A Book of Nursery Songs and Rhymes. With Illustrations by Members of the Birmingham Art School under the Direction of A. J. Gaskin. *London: Methuen & Company, Essex St. Strand.* 1879.

The collection benefits from Baring-Gould's wide interest in literature, in antiquarian matters, and in folksong, of which he was a pioneer collector. The volume itself, with its heavily decorated pages in William Morris style, could qualify for inclusion among period collections.

52 GRACE RHYS. Cradle Songs and Nursery Rhymes. *London: Walter Scott, Limited, Paternoster Square. New York: 3 East Fourteenth Street.* 1894

Although this collection was made principally from printed sources, the editor saw the rhymes afresh, making evident their poetry, vitality, and universality. This copy has pleasant associations. It was inscribed in 1895 to the painter Louise Starr by Countess Martenengo-Cesaresco, whose book on folksongs is the source of some of the lullabies; and Louise Starr's daughter Estella Canziani, whose picture 'The Piper of Dreams' hung in our nurseries, and in innumerable other nurseries in the 1920s, gave it to us.

53 FRANK KIDSON. 75 British Nursery Rhymes (And a Collection of Old Jingles). With Pianoforte Accompaniment by Alfred Moffat. *London: Augener Limited, Regent Street & Newgate Street.* [1904]

An excellent collection of rhymes 'with the melodies which have always been associated with them'.

54 R. J. MACLENNAN. Scottish Nursery Rhymes. Illustrated by Louis Mackay. *London: Andrew Melrose, 3 York Street, Covent Garden.* 1909

An attractive collection, apparently not beholden to Chambers (no. 39).

55 [L. EDNA WALTER] Mother Goose's Nursery Rhymes. Complete Edition. Containing Eight Full-Page Illustrations in Colour and Numerous Illustrations in the Text. *A. & C. Black, Ltd., 4, 5, & 6 Soho Square, London, W.1.*

1928 edition of a collection, first published in 1919, which is notable more for the quantity of rhymes included than the quality. The editor had

scruples (unlike some book makers) about including other people's copyright collectings. A number of verses are given as they appeared in chapbooks of the first half of the nineteenth century; but although the collection has been many times reprinted it has not succeeded in resuscitating them. The collection was originally illustrated by Folkard in the text. In 1924 four colour plates were added (very much of their period) by D. M. Wheelen, and in 1928 four more. In 1930 they were replaced with colour plates by Folkard. This edition is also shown. The text remains unaltered.

56 CECIL SHARP. Nursery Songs from the Appalachian Mountains. Arranged with Pianoforte Accompaniment by Cecil J. Sharp. Illustrated in Silhouette by Esther B. Mackinnon. *London: Novello & Company, Ltd., 160 Wardour St., W.1.* [1921 and 1923]

2 vols. First and Second Series. A selection of nursery songs from the great folksong collection made by Cecil Sharp and Maud Karpeles, which was published in *English Folk Songs from the Southern Appalachians*, 1917 and 1932.

57 [ROBERT GRAVES] The Less Familiar Nursery Rhymes. The Augustan Books of English Poetry, Second Series, Number Fourteen. *London: Ernest Benn Ltd., Bouverie House, Fleet Street.* [1927]

One of the few collections to have been made by a poet; and, from an aesthetic point of view, one of the most satisfactory of all collections. With the pamphlet are letters from Graves on the sources of his rhymes.

58 NICHT AT EENIE the Bairns' Parnassus, with wood-engravings by Iain MacNab. *Samson Press:* 1932.

A collection of about 70 rhymes almost all from oral collection or recollection. One of an edition of 170 copies; together with letters about the work from one of the editor-printers, Miss J. M. Shelmerdine.

59 NORAH & WILLIAM MONT-GOMERIE. Sandy Candy And Other Scottish Nursery Rhymes. Illustrated by Norah Montgomerie. *The Hogarth Press Ltd., 40–42 William IV Street, London, W.C.2.* 1948.

Nearly all the 345 rhymes in this pleasant collection were assembled from sources other than Chambers (no. 39 above). Part of the collection was subsequently reprinted in *The Hogarth Book of Scottish Nursery Rhymes* (1964), by the same editors.

60 BERNARD SHAW'S NURSERY RHYMES. 8/6/1950

Signed typescript. During the years the *Oxford Dictionary of Nursery Rhymes* was being prepared the editors were often encouraged by the contributions of well-wishers. One of them was Shaw, who sent these recollections, including a song he said he composed himself to sing 'when petting our dog Rover. It was my Opus 1.

Dumpitydoodledum big bowwow
Dumpitydoodledum dandy.'

This document may perhaps be allowed to stand for the several thousand contributions which have been received over the years, and which are preserved in our archives.

---

61 IONA and PETER OPIE. The Oxford Nursery Rhyme Book. With additional illustrations by Joan Hassall. *Oxford: At the Clarendon Press.* 1955

This book brings together 800 rhymes, the versions being selected from the material accumulated during the preparation of *The Oxford Dictionary of Nursery Rhymes* (no. 642), and also from the rhymes subsequently sent by readers in the great days when it became almost a national sport to find verses the *Dictionary* did not include. Some of the 130 sources of the illustrations are to be seen elsewhere in the exhibition. The originals of the 150 illustrations by Joan Hassall are also on view.

62 IONA and PETER OPIE. The Puffin Book of Nursery Rhymes. With illustrations by Pauline Baynes. *Penguin Books.* 1963

Two hundred of the 350 rhymes in this collection are additional to those appearing in *The Oxford Nursery Rhyme Book*, or are distinctly different versions. The two volumes together thus make a collection of a thousand traditional rhymes. On view also are the originals of Pauline Baynes's illustrations. In the United States a hardcover edition of this volume is published by the Oxford University Press, titled *A Family Book of Nursery Rhymes*.

3 Popular and Period Collections

Most of these popular collections were produced for a mass market. They relied for their success, as such collections still do, on their cheapness, their colourfulness, their availability, and on that perennial attrac-tion, the familiarity of their contents. They were produced unselfconsciously, without thought that any copies would be preserved, and documented, and judged by a later age. They therefore reflect the times in which they were produced with mirror-like accuracy. They are a genuine substratum of social archaeology. Even the twopenny midget books of the 1940s evoke the days of effort and austerity in a way no war history can do. And we are preserving popular publications of the present day for the same reason: so that a future generation can know about the 1970s. The more ambitious collections, we feel, can be left to look after themselves. But we do show here several gift books, novelty books, and special editions, chiefly of the nineteenth century, which also, in one way or another, reflect the taste of their time, if only among the well-to-do.

Lovers of folksong may like to know that a good few of the chapbooks here, printed in Leeds and the West Riding, were the gift of the venerated folksong collector Aunt Anne Gilchrist, who in turn was given them by Frank Kidson, another great tune man (see 75 British Nursery Rhymes, no. 53), who bought them 'new' in small newsagents at the end of the last century. A further number of ephemeral collections, published in the 1960s, have been the gift of Miss Carrol Jenkins.

63 CHILDREN'S TALES or Infant Prattle. *London: Published Septr 1, 1818 by J. Bysh, No. 52 Paternoster Row and Sold by C. Penny, Wood Street.*

A modest collection of ten rhymes, each with a hand-coloured illustration. Text and illustrations engraved throughout. Pages $3^7/_{10} \times 3\frac{1}{2}$ ins.

64 THE CHEERFUL WARBLER, or Juvenile Song Book. *York: Printed and Sold by J. Kendrew, Colliergate.* [c. 1820]

A 16 pp. nursery rhyme chapbook notable for the number of references it contains to drink.

65 NURSE LOVECHILD'S LEGACY. *London. Printed & sold by T. Batchelar, 14 Hackney Road Crescent.* [c. 1825]

A 16 pp. chapbook.

66 THE SUGAR PLUM. *Leeds: J. Roberts, 4, Wood-street.* [c. 1825]

A collection of eight nursery rhymes.

67 A COLLECTION OF BIRDS & RIDDLES. By Miss Polly & Master Tommy. *York: J. Kendrew, Printer, Colliergate.* [c. 1825]

A 16 pp. chapbook.

68 NURSERY RHYMES FOR CHILDREN. *Alnwick: Published by W. Davison.* One Halfpenny. [c. 1830]

An 8 pp. chapbook in which several of the rhymes are illustrated with vignettes by Bewick, engraved originally for subjects quite unrelated to nursery rhymes.

69 THE NURSERY RHYME QUADRIL- LES, for the Piano Forte by L. A. Shury. *London, Printed by W. Wybrow, 33 Rathbone Place, and Sold by all Book & Music Sellers in the United Kingdom.* [c. 1830]

70 JACK HORNER'S PRETTY TOY. *London: Printed and sold by J. E. Evans, Long Lane, Smithfield.* [c. 1830]

An early example of the name of a nursery rhyme character being used to sponsor a miscellany.

71 NURSERY RHYMES. *London: W. S. Johnson, Printer and Publisher, St. Martin's Lane, Charing Cross.* [c. 1830]

The woodcuts date back to about 1800. See *Oxford Nursery Rhyme Book,* pp. 212 and 214.

72 CRADLE MELODIES. [*Printed by Thomas Richardson, Derby.* c. 1830]

12 pp. Size 3⅝ × 2 ins.

73 THE RIDDLER'S RIDDLE BOOK; or a Choice Collection of Riddles. By Peter Puzzlecap, Esq. The little Rhyming Riddler. *Banbury: Printed and Sold by J. G. Rusher, Bridge-Street.* Price One Penny. [c. 1830]

74 NURSERY RHYMES. *London: Printed by J. McGowan, Great Windmill Street; for J. Bysh, 8, Cloth Fair, West-Smithfield.* Price Sixpence. [c. 1831]

75 NURSERY RHYMES. Embellished with beautiful Engravings. *London: John Bysh, 8, Cloth Fair, West-Smithfield.* Price Sixpence. [c. 1835]

This booklet contains Hodgson's edition of 'Nursery Rhymes for Good Children', and has no connection with no. 74. The hand-coloured illustrations are enlarged with three-colour decor- ative borders.

76 CRADLE MELODIES. [*Devonport: Printed by S. & J. Keys.* c. 1835]

Advertised for sale at one half-penny.

77 THE INFANT'S OWN BOOK: or a collection of The Old and Amusing Favourites . . . with Nearly 150 Illustrative Engravings. Neatly Coloured: To which is added The Popular Ditties . . . Third Edition. *London: D. Carvalho, 74, Chiswell Street, Finsbury Square.* [c. 1835]

Eleven of Carvalho's booklets, such as 'Tom the Piper's Son', 'The House that Jack built', and 'Jack and Jill, and Old Dame Gill', have been bound together in printed boards to make a bumper volume.

78 PUZZLECAP'S AMUSING RIDDLE BOOK. [*Devonport: Printed by S. & J. Keys.* c. 1835]

A collection of rhyming riddles advertised for sale at one half-penny.

79 SONGS FOR LITTLE CHILDREN. *Bishop & Co., Printers, 101, Houndsditch, London.* [c. 1840]

8 pp. chapbook, the first page hand-coloured.

80 NURSERY RHYMES. *London: Printed for the Booksellers.* [c. 1840]

Chapbook, with publisher's hand-coloured illus- trations on four of the eight pages.

81 NURSERY RHYMES. *London: Richardson and Son, 172, Fleet St.; 9, Capel Street, Dublin; and Derby.* Price One Penny. [c. 1840]

82 THE PUZZLE-CAP: A Collection of Riddles, Unriddled for your entertainment At the Fire Side. *Derby: Printed by and for Henry Mozley and Son.* Price One Penny. [c. 1840]

83 THE RIDDLE BOOK; or, Fireside Amuse- ments. *London: Richardson and Son, 172, Fleet St.; 9, Capel Street, Dublin; and Derby.* Price One Penny. [c. 1840]

Contains 22 rhyming riddles, each with a pictorial answer.

84 LONDON JINGLES AND COUNTRY TALES, for Young People. *Banbury: Printed by J. G. Rusher.* [c. 1840]

85 NURSERY POEMS, from the Ancient and Modern Poets. *Banbury: Printed by J. G. Rusher.* [c. 1840]

The chapbook is unfolded to show how the sixteen pages are printed on a single sheet.

86 NURSERY RHYMES, from the Royal Collections. *Banbury: Printed by J. G. Rusher.* [c. 1840]

87 POETIC TRIFLES, for Young Gentlemen & Ladies. *Banbury: Printed by J. G. Rusher.* [c. 1840]

88 THE NURSERY RHYMES, Illustrated. Mark's Edition. *London: Published by J. L. Marks, Long Lane, Smithfield.* [c. 1840]

The lively engravings, two to a page, are hand-coloured.

89 THE ROYAL INFANT OPERA, Composed expressly for His Royal Highness The Prince of Wales, & Inscribed to Every British Mother by O. B. Dussek. *London. D'Almaine & Co. 20, Soho Square.* [1841]

The Second Royal Infant Opera . . . [1842]

The two 'Operas' contain thirty-one nursery songs between them. The lithographed pictorial covers are by William Buckley.

90 THE NURSERY QUADRILLES. Composed by J. Blewitt. *London: Robert Cocks & Co., New Burlington Street.* [c. 1845]

91 THE NURSERY RHYMES. *Shearcroft, Printer, Braintree.* [c. 1845]

An 8 pp. chapbook.

92 NURSERY DITTIES. *London: Printed and Sold by J. T. Wood, 278, Strand.* [c. 1845]

An 8 pp. chapbook utilising woodcuts of an earlier date.

93 NURSERY RHYMES. *London; Printed and Sold by J. T. Wood, 278, Strand.* [c. 1845]

A pair to Wood's Nursery Ditties.

94 NURSERY RHYMES. *Printed by W. S. Johnson, 60, St. Martin's Lane, Charing Cross.* [c. 1845].

An 8 pp. chapbook containing thirty-four rhymes.

95 NURSERY RHYMES. *London: Webb, Millington and Co., Wine-Office Court, Fleet-Street. Also, Leeds and Otley.* [c. 1845]

A chapbook containing a number of Scots rhymes.

96 CRADLE RHYMES FOR INFANTS. *John and Charles Mozley, Derby; and Paternoster Row, London. Price One Halfpenny.* [c. 1850]

97 NURSERY RHYMES. *London: Published by A. Park, 47, Leonard Street, Finsbury. Price Three-pence.* [c. 1850]

In Park's Library of Instruction and Amusement. Hand-coloured illustrations.

98 HARRY'S LADDER TO LEARNING. With Two Hundred and Thirty Illustrations. *London: David Bogue, 86 Fleet Street.* [c. 1850].

In six parts. Parts III and IV, Harry's Nursery Songs and Harry's Nursery Tales, contain nursery rhymes.

99 ILLUSTRATED DITTIES OF YE OLDEN TIME. With Steel Engravings. *London: Dean & Son, Ludgate Hill.* [1851 ?]

An early Victorian gift book. Text and illustrations engraved throughout. Bound in bevelled boards, with rich gilt decoration on front cover.

100 AUNT MAVOR'S BOOK OF NURSERY RHYMES. *Geo. Routledge & Co., London & New York.* [1856]

One of Aunt Mavor's Little Library. Price six-pence; or, with the plates coloured, one shilling. Illustrated by William McConnell.

101 MOTHER HUBBARD, and Other Old Friends. By Brother Sunshine. *Dean & Son, Juvenile Publication Warehouse, 31, Ludgate-Hill, Three Doors from Old Bailey.* [c. 1858]

The other old friends include Cock Robin, Old King Cole, The Queen of Hearts, and Little Jack Horner. Large hand-coloured illustrations throughout. The price was 3s. 6d.

102 ROUTLEDGE'S NURSERY PICTURE BOOK, Containing Upwards of Six Hundred and Thirty Illustrations. *London: Routledge, Warne, and Routledge, Farringdon Street; and 56, Walker Street, New York.* 1862

In this bumper five shilling book, with pages $12\frac{1}{2} \times 9\frac{3}{4}$ ins, the nursery rhyme section has pictures by William McConnell, Harrison Weir, and others. All the pictures originally appeared in other publications.

103 THE NURSERY PLAYMATE, Illustrated with More Than Two Hundred Engravings. *London: Sampson Low, Son, & Marston, 47 Ludgate Hill. 1864.*

The contents are chiefly from Joseph Cundall's *Pleasure Books*, with the addition of E. V. Boyle's *Child's Play*, and material from Felix Summerly's *Home Treasury*.

104 THE CHILD'S PICTURE STORY BOOK; with Four Hundred Illustrations by John Gilbert, J. D. Watson, W. M'Connell, Harrison Weir, W. Harvey, &c., &c. *London: Routledge, Warne, and Routledge, Broadway, Ludgate Hill.* 1865

Eight titles including 'Nursery Rhymes', 'The History of Five Little Pigs', and 'The History of the Little Old Woman who lived in a Shoe', previously published separately, brought together in one volume 'as a Gift or Reward for the Good Little Ones'.

105 NURSERY RHYMES. *Goode Bros. Printers & Publishers, Clerkenwell Green, London E.C.* [c. 1865]

Consists of a single sheet, $17 \times 13\frac{1}{2}$ ins, folded twice to make eight pages.

106 NURSERY RHYMES. *London: Frederick Warne & Co.* [c. 1865]

The third (as yet unnumbered) of Aunt Louisa's London Toy Books.

107 AUNT LOUISA'S LONDON PICTURE BOOK. Comprising A. Apple Pie. The Railway A.B.C. Nursery Rhymes. With Eighteen Pages of Illustrations, Printed in Colours by Kronheim. *Frederick Warne and Co. Bedford Street, Covent Garden.* 1866

The first composite volume of Aunt Louisa's London Toy Books. Bound in crimson cloth, with an amount of gilt decoration.

108 AUNT LOUISA'S LONDON PICTURE BOOK. Comprising A. Apple Pie. Nursery Rhymes. The Railway A.B.C. Childhood's Happy Hours. With Twenty-four Pages of Illustrations, Printed in Colours by Kronheim and Evans. *London: Frederick Warne and Co., Bedford Street, Covent Garden. New York: Scribner and Co.* 1867

In this edition, which is similarly bound in crimson cloth, a fourth title has been added, *Childhood's Happy Hours.*

109 AUNT FRIENDLY'S GIFT. Containing Seventy-Two Pages of Pictures Printed in Colours, with Letter-Press Descriptions. *London: Frederick Warne and Co., Bedford Street, Covent Garden. New York: Scribner, Welford, and Co.* [1867]

The volume consists of the first twelve of Aunt Friendly's 3d. Toy Books, amongst them 'Nursery Songs', 'Nursery Ditties', 'Cock Robin' (illustrated by Walter Crane), and 'The House that Jack Built' (see no. 411). Two copies are possessed. The one in blue cloth, with embossed decoration on front cover, appearing to be the earlier.

110 CHILDREN'S LULLABIES. *London: Frederick Warne & Co.* [c. 1867]

Aunt Louisa's London Toy Books, no. 32. The illustrations are particularly pleasing examples of the colour printing of Kronheim & Co.

111 AUNT LOUISA'S KEEPSAKE. Comprising Sing a Song o' Sixpence. The Robin's Christmas Eve. Robin Hood & his Merry Men. The Sea Side. With Twenty-four Pages of Illustrations, Printed in Oil Colours by Kronheim and Dalziels. *London: Frederick Warne and Co., Bedford Street, Covent Garden. New York: Scribner, Welford, and Co.* 1868

Bound in crimson cloth, the gilt and blind-stamp decoration being even more extensive than in 1866 and 1867.

112 OLD NURSERY SONGS, STORIES, AND BALLADS. With Numerous Illustrations by Eminent Modern Artists, and Eight Coloured Engravings. *London: Ward, Lock & Tyler, Warwick House, Paternoster Row.* [1869]

The eight poorly-reproduced colour illustrations are from 'The Home Treasury', including *Traditional Nursery Songs*, 1843 (no. 236)

113 NATIONAL NURSERY RHYMES AND NURSERY SONGS. Set to Original Music by J. W. Elliott. With Illustrations, Engraved by the Brothers Dalziel. *London: George Routledge and Sons, Broadway, Ludgate Hill. Glasgow, Manchester, and New York. Novello, Ewer, and Co., Berners Street, W., and 35 Poultry, E.C.* [1870]

The engravings are after original designs by Griset, Marks, Pinwell, Zwecker, Arthur Hughes, and other well-known artists. The volume was reprinted many times, and, considering the price was 7s. 6d., its sale was enormous.

114 AUNT FRIENDLY'S NURSERY KEEP-SAKE. Containing Seventy-Two Pages of Pictures Printed in Colours by Kronheim. With Letter-Press Descriptions. *London: Frederick Warne and Co., Bedford Street, Covent Garden. New York: Scribner, Welford and Armstrong.* [c. 1870]

'Sing-a-song of sixpence' and 'The Frog who would a wooing go' are amongst the twelve nursery stories brought together here.

115 AUNT FRIENDLY'S NURSERY GIFT BOOK. Containing Thirty-Six Pages of Pictures Printed in Colours by Dalziel Brothers. With Letter-Press Descriptions. *London: Frederick Warne and Co., Bedford Street, Covent Garden. New York: Scribner, Welford and Armstrong.* [c. 1870]

The volume consists of six of Aunt Friendly's 3d. Toy Books, four of which had already appeared in *Aunt Friendly's Gift* (no. 109), and two of which are new, 'Jack and Jill' and 'Cock Robin's Courtship'.

116 THE ROBIN REDBREAST PICTURE BOOK. With Forty-eight Pages of Illustrations. Printed in Colours by Kronheim & Co. *London and New York: George Routledge and Sons.* [1873]

'Nursery Rhymes' and 'My Mother' are two of the six titles brought together in this volume.

117 PUSSY'S PICTURE BOOK. With Thirty-Six Pages of Coloured Illustrations by Kronheim & Co. *London & New York: George Routledge and Sons.* [1874]

Six parts, also issued separately, among them 'Nursery Songs', 'Nursery Ditties', and 'The History of A Apple Pie'. A second copy is possessed with a later imprint *London: George Routledge and Sons, Broadway, Ludgate Hill. New York: 416 Broome Street.*

118 TOTTIE'S NURSERY RHYMES. *London: Frederick Warne & Co.* [1875?]

Aunt Louisa's London Toy Books, no. 69. The illustrations are after designs by M. Tilsley. Compare the title-page with Dean's *Nursery Rhymes ABC* published some twenty years later.

119 A SINGING QUADRILLE. Composed for the Piano Forte, by Cotsford Dick. *London: Robert Cocks & Co. New Burlington St. Regent St. W, Music Publishers to Her Majesty Queen Victoria, & His Royal Highness the Prince of Wales.* [c. 1875]

Sheet music with coloured lithographed cover by Alfred Concanen showing six nursery rhymes.

120 COCK ROBIN, and Other Nursery Tales. With Twenty-Four Page Illustrations, Printed in Colours. *London: Frederick Warne and Co. Bedford Street, Strand. New York: Scribner, Welford and Armstrong.* [c. 1875]

One of Warne's 'Now and Then' Juvenile Series, but the contents, such as Walter Crane's 'Cock Robin', come from Aunt Friendly's Toy Books.

121 PUSS IN BOOTS and other Nursery Tales. With Thirty-Six Page Illustrations Printed in Colours. *London: Frederick Warne & Co., Bedford Street, Strand.* [c. 1875]

Warne's 'Now and Then' Juvenile Series. Includes 'The Story of the Three Little Pigs,' 'The Frog Who Would A Wooing Go,' 'Dame Trot and her Cat,' 'Sing-a-Song of Sixpence,' and 'Tom Thumb,' all with full-page colour illustrations.

122 RIDICULA REDIVIVA. By J. E. Rogers. Printed in Colours by R. Clay, Sons, and Taylor. *London: Macmillan and Co.* 1876

First published 1868, dated 1869. Also issued in four paper-cover shilling parts, one of which (no. 3), is shown alongside. The brightly coloured illustrations depict a pseudo medieval period in the manner of H. S. Marks.

123 THE OLD FASHIONED MOTHER GOOSE' MELODIES, Complete with Magic Colored Pictures. *G. W. Carleton & Co., Publishers; Donaldson Brothers, Designers & Printers.* 1879

Illustrated by William Ludwell Sheppard. Each picture has a flap which, when turned over, reveals a further development in the story. For instance the pie set before the king is opened and shown to be full of blackbirds. The volume contains the six numbers of the Magic Mother Goose series, which were also sold separately. See no. 537.

124 LIVING NURSERY RHYMES newly treated with Moving Pictures. By Mrs M. J. Wells. *Dean & Son, 160A Fleet St.* [1879]

One of Dean's New Surprise Picture Books. The characters in the pictures are made to move by pulling tabs. On the page shown the Queen lifts a spoonful of honey, while the King lowers his hand to count his gold.

125 AUNT LOUISA'S OLD NURSERY FRIENDS. With Full-Page Illustrations from Original Designs. Printed in Colours. *London and New York: Frederick Warne and Co.* [c. 1880]

One of Aunt Louisa's Coloured Gift Books, containing Cinderella, Dame Trot, and Old Mother Hubbard.

126 AUNT LOUISA'S OUR FAVOURITES. Comprising Cock Robin's Life and Death. Dame Trot. Punch and Judy. With Full-page Illustrations from Original Designs. Printed in Colours by Kronheim. *London and New York: Frederick Warne and Co.* [c. 1880].

One of Aunt Louisa's Coloured Gift Books.

127 AUNT LOUISA'S GOLDEN GIFT. Comprising Little Dame Crump. Hush-a-Bye Baby. Childhood's Delight. Tottie's Nursery Rhymes. With Twenty-four Pages of Illustrations, Printed in Colours and Gold, From Original Designs by M. Tilsey. *London: Frederick Warne and Co., Bedford Street, Strand.* [c. 1880]

A book that lives up to its title. Gold is used lavishly in the illustrations.

128 LITTLE DANCES FOR LITTLE DANCERS. *London: H. D'Alcorn, 25 Poland St., Oxford St., W.* [c. 1880]

A medley of nursery tunes.

129 OLD FAVOURITES. *London: Frederick Warne & Co.* [c. 1885]

Aunt Louisa's London Toy Books, no. 105. The illustrations are much influenced by Kate Greenaway.

130 NURSERY RHYMES. The Queen of Hearts, &c. *T. Nelson & Sons, London & Edinburgh.* [c. 1885]

131 THE GOLDEN PLAYBOOK, Comprising The Golden Alphabet, Dorothy's Dolls, and Red Riding Hood's Party. With Original Illustrations by Alfred J. Johnson. Printed in Gold and Colours by Edmund Evans. *London and New York: Frederick Warne and Co.* 1886.

The Golden A.B.C. features personalities from nursery rhymes and fairy tales.

132 BO-PEEP MOTHER GOOSE MELODIES. *New-York: McLoughlin Bros.* Copyrighted 1887.

Printed on linen. The collection principally depicts the disasters and unpleasantnesses occurring in the nursery rhymes. Even the 'little pig who cried wee, wee,' is shown to be coming home drunk.

133 OLD FRIENDS WITH NEW FACES, illustrated by Will Gibbons. *Castell Brothers. London: E. & J. B. Young & Co. New York.* [1888]

134 NURSERY RHYMES. With 117 Illustrations by W. McConnell. *London: George Routledge and Sons, Limited, Broadway, Ludgate Hill. Glasgow, Manchester and New York.* [1890]

This edition is No. 11 in the Master Jack series, The book was first published c. 1860.

135 MOTHER GOOSE'S NURSERY RHYMES, TALES AND JINGLES, With 400 Illustrations. *London: Frederick Warne and Co. and New York.* [1890]

Probably the best-selling family nursery rhyme book at the end of the nineteenth century. The publishers, 'as proprietors of "Nursery Rhymes, Tales, and Jingles", "Popular Nursery Tales", and Halliwell's "Nursery Rhymes and Tales" . . . considered [it] advisable to embody the whole in one exhaustive volume'.

136 YOUNG ENGLAND'S NURSERY RHYMES. Illustrated by Constance Haslewood. *London & New York: Frederick Warne & Co.* [1890]

Two copies: one in cloth-covered bevelled boards, gilt; the other in paper-covered boards. The first shows Bo-peep; the second My Pretty Maid, and has a pictorial advertisement on back cover for Cha's Baker & Co's Boys' Sailor Suits.

137 YOUNG ENGLAND'S PAINTING BOOK. By Constance Haslewood. Containing 32 Outline Pictures for Water Colour Painting and A Fully Coloured Copy for each. *London & New York: Frederick Warne & Co.* [1890]

The pictures are from *Young England's Nursery Rhymes*, two to a page. Gift of Miss Doreen Gullen.

138 NURSERY RHYMES ABC. *London: Printed & Published by Dean & Son, 160a, Fleet Street, E.C.* [c.1890]

No. 11 in Dean's Gold Medal Series. The cover is clearly intended to appeal as much to the fashionable mother, who might purchase the book, as to the child.

139 FAVOURITE RHYMES AND RIDDLES, Two Volumes in One. *T. Nelson and Sons: London, Edinburgh, and New York.* 1892.

This volume comprises *Favourite Rhymes for the Nursery*, 1892, and *Riddles and Rhymes*, 1892.

140 AUNT LOUISA'S BOOK OF NURSERY RHYMES, With Numerous Illustrations. *London: Frederick Warne and Co. and New York.* [1892]

One of Aunt Louisa's Favourite Instruction Books.

141 NATIONAL RHYMES OF THE NURSERY, With Introduction by George Saintsbury, and Drawings by Gordon Browne. *London: Wells Gardner Darton & Co., 3 Paternoster Buildings, E.C.* [1895]

142 NURSERY RHYMES. With Original Pen and Ink Drawings. Books for the Bairns.—III. Edited by W. T. Stead. *London: 'Review of Reviews' Office.* [1896]

'Price One Penny'.

143 MORE NURSERY RHYMES. With Entirely New Illustrations by Brinsley Le Fanu. Books for the Bairns.—XIX. Edited by W. T. Stead. *London: 'Review of Reviews' Office.* [c. 1897]

W. T. Stead, a man who gave his heart and mind to every detail of his publishing business, has here changed 'rascally Jew' in the rhyme of Mother Goose to 'rascally Screw', saying that had he not done so he 'might have hurt the feelings of many good people who have been most cruelly used for nearly two thousand years'.

144 FATHER TUCK'S TINY TOTS' SERIES. Little Bo-peep. Little Jack Horner. *Raphael Tuck & Sons, Ltd. Publishers to the Queen, London-Paris-New York.* [c. 1897]

Two eight-page glossy booklets, 6½ × 4¼ ins., each containing a number of rhymes. The gift of Miss G. Rogers-Tillstone.

145 MOTHER GOOSE'S ABC. Untearable. *London: Ernest Nister. New York: E. P. Dutton.* [c. 1900]

146 ONE TWO BUCKLE MY SHOE. *London: Ernest Nister. New York: E. P. Dutton & Co.* [1901 ?]

A book of number rhymes, illustrated by E. S. Hardy, with line drawings, and four coloured plates which were also issued as a boxed set of jigsaw puzzles (see amongst nursery rhyme novelties).

147 A BOOK OF NURSERY RHYMES. Being Mother Goose's Melodies Arranged in the Order of Attractiveness and Interest. By Charles Welsh.

With One Hundred and Seventy Illustrations by Clara E. Atwood. Part I [Part II] *London: Society for Promoting Christian Knowledge, Northumberland Avenue, W.C.; 43, Queen Victoria Street, E.C. Brighton: 129, North Street.* 1902.

Arranged in categories: 'Mother Play', 'Mother Stories', 'Child Play', 'Child Stories', &c.

148 OLD NURSERY RHYMES DUG UP AT THE PYRAMIDS. By Stanley L. Adamson. The Additional Verses by Oliver Booth. *London: Dean & Son, Ltd., 160a, Fleet Street, E.C.* [1903]

The book is presented as an archaeological find, with sackcloth binding, and a ribbon tie sealed with an official-looking 'Dean & Son Limited' seal. The pictures are in Egyptian style, but, except for Boy Blue who is employed by an Egyptian farmer, the extended nursery rhymes remain firmly based in the British Isles.

149 MY NURSERY RHYME BOOK. *Ernest Nister, London, & E. P. Dutton & Co. New York.* [c. 1910]

150 NURSERY RHYMES A.B.C. *Valentine & Sons Ltd.* [c. 1910]

151 A NURSERY MEDLEY. Set to Music by Violet Gardiner. Illustrated by Alix Grein. *London: Chapman & Hall, Limited.* [c. 1910]

152 MUSICAL NURSERY RHYMES. Dean's Pictureland Series, No. 1, *London: Dean & Son Limited, 160A Fleet Street.* [c. 1910]

Illustrated by Ethel K. Burgess.

153 OUR NURSERY RHYME BOOK. Edited by Letty and Frank Littlewood. Illustrated by Honor C. Appleton. *London: Simpkin, Marshall, Hamilton, Kent & Co., Ltd. 4 Stationers' Hall Court, E.C.* [1912]

The editors were aged three and six, as explained in the preface by 'S.R.L.' (Samuel Robinson Littlewood).

154 MOTHER GOOSE. Pictured by Willy Pogány. *London: George G. Harrap & Company Limited.* [1915]

155 MOTHER GOOSE RHYMES. Pictured by Willy Pogány. *London: George G. Harrap & Company Limited.* [1915]

156 OUR FAVOURITE NURSERY SONGS. With Full Page Illustrations on Every Alternate Page. *London: Frederick Warne & Co. Ltd. and New York.* [c. 1915]

Open at an unusually realistic picture of the maid in 'Sing a Song of Sixpence' having her nose sewn on again.

157 NURSERY SONGS. 'The Chimney Corner' Series *Sam'l Gabriel Sons & Company, New York.* [1916]

Illustrations by Mary LaFetra Russell.

158 THE ANIMAL BUBBLE BOOK, Hodder Columbia Books that Sing, Three Little Kittens. Three Little Piggies. Three Blind Mice. Story by Ralph Mayhew and Burges Johnson. Pictures by Rhoda Chase. Records by Columbia Gramophone Co. *Hodder and Stoughton Limited, London, Publishers.* [1918]

A pictorial album containing three records.

159 THE LITTLE BOOK OF NURSERY RHYMES. Illustrated by Flora White. *Sevenoaks: Printed and Published by J. Salmon.* [c. 1920]

Bound with thread knotted in a bow. The illustrations mounted.

160 RHYME TIME. 'A Collins Picture Book' [c. 1920]

161 MOTHER GOOSE PRIMER for Reading and Colouring. By A. M. Goode. *George G. Harrap & Co. Ltd. London. Calcutta. Sydney.* [1922]

162 OLD ENGLISH NURSERY SONGS. Music Arranged by Horace Mansion. Pictured by Anne Anderson. *London: George G. Harrap & Co. Ltd, and at Sydney.* [1922?]

163 FATHER TUCK'S NURSERY FRIENDS. *Raphael Tuck & Son, Ltd., London, Paris, New York.* [c. 1925]

164 FATHER TUCK'S NURSERY FAVOURITES. *Raphael Tuck & Son, Ltd., London, Paris, New York.* [c. 1925]

165 NURSERY RHYMES. *The Royal Series.* [c. 1925].

An 'Untearable' collection, illustrated by H. G. C. Marsh Lambert, and published at 6d.

166 BETTY BLUE. Dean's Pinafore Series No. 5. *Dean & Son Ltd., Debrett House, 29 King Street, Covent Garden, London W.C.2.* [c. 1925]

167 NURSERY RHYMES. Illustrated with Six Woodcuts, Hand Coloured, By M. Alleyne. *Printed by H. Gilead Smith and published at the Saint Loup Press, Sanremo, Italy.* 1926

Edition limited to one hundred copies, of which this is no. 99. Signed by the artist.

168 OLD NURSERY RHYMES. With pictures by Ethel Everett. *T. C. & E. C. Jack Ltd.* [1927]

The illustrations apparently influenced by Lovat Fraser.

169 OLD RHYMES FOR ALL TIMES. Collected and Illustrated by Cicely Mary Barker. *Blackie & Son Limited: London and Glasgow.* [1928]

170 MOTHER GOOSE. The Old Favourite Nursery Rhymes. Illustrated by Margaret W. Tarrant. *Ward, Lock & Company, Limited, London and Melbourne.* [c. 1930]

No. 1 of The Little Wonder Books.

171 MOTHER GOOSE RHYMES. Illustrated by Ismena Mermagen. *The Children's Press, London and Glasgow.* [c. 1930]

One of the small dumpy books typical of the period.

172 OLD NURSERY RHYMES. *Thomas Nelson and Sons Ltd.* [c. 1930]

Illustrations by Jack Orr.

173 NURSERY PICTURES. *Thomas Nelson and Sons, Ltd. London, Edinburgh, New York, Toronto, and Paris.* [c. 1930]

Illustrated by Jack Orr.

174 THE CHILDREN'S SONG BOOK with Coloured Illustrations. Edited by Alfred W. Tomlyn Mus. Bac. *Edinburgh: Andersons Limited.* [1932]

Bound in colour-printed linen of nursery design.

175 THE LONDON TREASURY OF NURSERY RHYMES. Collected by J. Murray MacBain, Associate Editor of Child Education. *University of London Press, Ltd. 10 & 11 Warwick Lane, London, E.C.4.* [1933]

In addition to nursery rhymes the volume includes a number of poems written for children although given anonymously.

176 LITTLE FOLKS' BOOK OF NURSERY RHYMES. *Frederick Warne & Co., Ltd. London and New York.* [1936]

The illustrations reflect the period. The Queen of Hearts, for all her crown, is instantly recognisable as a 1930s housewife.

177 PLAYTIME NURSERY RHYMES. [*Valentine & Sons, Ltd., Dundee & London.* c. 1938. Price about 4d.]

178 A BOOK OF NURSERY RHYMES. Illustrated by Enid Marx. *Chatto and Windus: London.* 1939

179 A BOOK OF NURSERY RHYMES. Illustrated by Enid Marx. *Zodiac Books: London.* 1949

A reissue published by Lighthouse Books.

180 THE LADYBIRD BOOK OF NURSERY RHYMES. Introduction by Auntie Muriel. Illustrations by Robert Knight. *Publishers: Wills & Hepworth Ltd., Loughborough.* [1941. Price 2/6]

181 15 NURSERY RHYMES with drawings by Clarke Hutton. A Puffin Picture Book. [1941]

182 FAVOURITE NURSERY RHYMES. Edited by Mrs. Herbert Strang. The Polly Wolly Books. *Humphrey Milford, Oxford University Press, London.* [1942]

Illustrations by Grace Lodge. Original Price 6d.

183 QUIZ. By Enid Marx. *Faber & Faber Ltd.* 1942

8 pp. midget booklet, $3\frac{1}{2} \times 2\frac{1}{2}$ ins., with a name-the-rhyme picture on each page. In printed gift envelope. Price 4d. Gift of Miss Pauline Baynes.

184 CHALLENGE MINIATURE BOOKS. Edited by Nan Dearmer. 1. All Things Bright and Beautiful. By Mrs. C. F. Alexander 1823–95. Illustrated by Olive F. Openshaw. 2. Now the Day is Over. By S. Baring Gould. Illustrated by Olive F. Openshaw. 3. I Saw Three Ships. Traditional Carol. Illustrated by Olive F. Openshaw. 9. Matthew Mark Luke and John. Anon. Illustrated and lithographed by Nora S. Unwin. [*The Challenge, 69, Gt. Peter Street, S.W.1., S.P.C.K. House, Northumberland Av., W.C.2.* 1943]

Four 12 pp. booklets. $3 \times 2\frac{1}{4}$ ins.

185 SYLVAN BOOKS. 1, 2, 4, 5. Pussy Cat, Pussy Cat. Hey Diddle Diddle. Tinker Tailor. Tom Tom the Piper's Son. All illustrated by John R. Biggs. 7. The News of the Day and Other Nursery Rhymes. Illustrated by B.B. 8. Humpty Dumpty and Other Nursery Rhymes. Illustrated by Biro. [*Sylvan Press, London.* c. 1943. Price 3d. each]

186 MOTHER GOOSE NURSERY RHYMES. *Raphael Tuck & Sons Ltd., London.* [c. 1943]

In Tuck's Better Little Book series, which included titles such as 'Life in the W.R.N.S.' and 'Love's Miracle'.

187 THE JOLLY JUMP-UPS MOTHER GOOSE BOOK. By Geraldine Clyne. *McLoughlin Bros., Inc. Springfield, Mass.* 1944

Three-dimensional pictures stand up when the book is opened. Gift of Miss Elisabeth Ball.

188 FAVOURITE NURSERY RHYMES. [*The Children's Press, London and Glasgow.* c. 1944]

Printed on grey wartime paper.

189 BANTAM PICTURE BOOKS. No. 18. The 12 Days of Christmas. Drawn by Margaret Levetus. [1944] No. 36. The Ploughboy in Luck. Illustrated by Marion Rivers-Moore. [1945] *Transatlantic Arts, Ltd., 45, Great Russell Street, London, W.C.1. and New York.*

190 PUFFIN RHYMES with drawings by John Harwood. [1945]

The third Baby Puffin Book published by Penguin Books Limited.

191 A BOOK OF RIGMAROLES or Jingle Rhymes. By Enid Marx. [1945]

Puffin Picture Books no. 12.

192 ANOTHER LOVELY BOOK OF NURSERY RHYMES. Pictures by Muriel Dawson. *Raphael Tuck & Sons Ltd.* [1945]

Price 4/6. The nursery rhyme characters are wearing the children's dungarees popular at the time.

193 LITTLE MISS MUFFET'S NURSERY RHYME BOOK. *Published & Printed by W. Walker & Sons (Associated) Ltd., 3 Woodstock St., London, W.1.* [c. 1945. Price 1/–]

194 OLD FAVOURITES, WITH PIC-
TURES FOR PAINTING. [*Harris Bros.
London W.1.* c. 1945]

A four-leaf concertina book on stiff board, the
pictures on one side left uncoloured for children to
paint.

195 NURSERY RHYME PARADE. Favourite
Nursery Rhyme Folk for Children's Scrap Books
and Nursery Decoration. Ready to Cut Out. On
Gummed Paper No Paste Needed. [Pitkin Picture
Book. c. 1945]

196 RHYME A RIDDLE. A Picture Book in
Colour Photography, by Paul Henning. Illustrating
rhymed riddles collected and edited by W. F.
Cuthbertson. *Guilford Press Limited, 2, Guilford
Place, London, W.C.1.* 1946

197 ONE TWO BUCKLE MY SHOE. Cloth
Lined. [Illustrated by Anne Rochester. *The R.A.
Publishing Co. Ltd., E.C.4.* c. 1946]

198 MOTHER GOOSE NURSERY RHYME
BOOK. MY PRETTY MAID BOOK OF
NURSERY RHYMES. THE PIPER'S SON
BOOK OF NURSERY RHYMES.

Three booklets purchased in Woolworth's Feb.
1947, price 3½d. each.

199 FIND THE NURSERY RHYME. A New
Playbook in Colour Photography. Figures and Sets
by Hugh and Sally Gee. *Published by Collins,
London, and Glasgow.* [1947]

Each rhyme is depicted in three strips and has to
be put together on the 'Heads, Bodies, and Tails'
principle.

200 COUNTING RHYMES. Illustrated by
Corinne Malvern. *Simon and Schuster, New York.*
[1947]

No. 12 in The Little Golden Library, a series
which had immense success after the war in Britain
as well as the U.S.A.

201 NURSERY RHYMES. MOTHER
GOOSE NURSERY RHYMES. Tiny Tuck
Books. [c. 1947. Price 2d. each.]

Two midget booklets, 3¾ × 2½ ins. Printed in
Canada.

202 IN NURSERY LAND. *Raphael Tuck &
Sons Ltd. London. New York. Toronto.* [A Father
Tuck Little Book. c. 1947. Price 1/6]

203 NURSERY NONSENSE. Arranged & Illustrated by Molly B. Thomson. [1948]

A "Kiddie Kut" book, published by Collins. The
pages are shaped and cut so that the pictures are
augmented by parts of the illustrations on other
pages.

204 A LITTLE MOTHER GOOSE. Illus-
trated by Janey Laura Scott. *Whitman Publishing
Co., Racine, Wisconsin.* 1949

205 NURSERY RHYMES. A Tom Thumb
Book. *Rand McNally & Company.* Printed in U.S.A.
[1949]

206 THE "MIGHTY MIDGETS" NUR-
SERY RHYMES No. 1 [No. 2]. *Published by W.
Barton (Publishers) Ltd., Central Street, London,
E.C.1.* [c. 1949]

3¾ × 2½ ins. Price 2d. each in Woolworth's.

207 DOROTHY STRACHEY BUSSY. Fifty
Nursery Rhymes. With a Commentary on English
Usage for French Students. *Gallimard.* [Paris 1950]

This collection, with its perceptive commentary,
quickly went into several impressions in France.
The mysteries of idiomatic English, says Madame
Bussy, can be learned through the medium of the
traditional nursery rhymes, 'whose jingles are so
catching, whose idioms are so familiar, whose words
are so common and essential'.

208 MY NURSERY RHYME BOOK. Pictures
by Muriel Dawson. [*Raphael Tuck & Sons Ltd.* A
Father Tuck Little Book. c. 1950. Price 1/6]

209 LULLABY RHYMES. [*Dean & Son Ltd.,
41/43 Ludgate Hill, London, E.C.4.* c. 1950]

Ten large full-colour pages printed on card for
2/-.

210 NURSERY SONGS. Arranged by Leah
Gale. Illustrated by Corinne Malvern. *Frederick
Muller Ltd,, London.* [c. 1950]

Little Golden Book no. 39. Originally published
by Simon and Schuster, Inc., 1949.

211 NURSERY RHYME PICTURES. Magic
Hidden Colour. Painting Without Paints. A
Chameleon Book. [*Juvenile Productions Ltd. London.*
c.1950]

212 MARY HAD A LITTLE LAMB and other
Nursery Songs. H. A. Rey. Puffin Picture Book 91.
[1951]

213 FAVOURITE NURSERY RHYMES. Real Fabric Pictures. Muse Arts "New Fabric" Series. [c. 1951]

> 'A book to feel as well as see
> Is certainly a novelty.'

214 NURSERY RHYMES. *The Children's Press —London & Glasgow.* [A Dinky Book. c. 1952. Price 3d.]

215 TEN LITTLE NURSERY RHYMES. *Raphael Tuck & Sons Ltd.* [1953]

Illustrated by 'Dinah'. The cover simulates a television set, and the heads of the nursery rhyme characters depicted inside can be seen through the cut-out screen.

216 SING A SONG OF SIXPENCE and other Nursery Rhymes, All with Transfer Pictures. *Published by W.H.C. London* No. 43. [1953]

Five pages of rhymes and 48 small square transfers.

217 NURSERY RHYMES with "Come-to-Life" pictures. *Raphael Tuck & Sons Ltd. Fine Art Publishers by Appointment to the Late King George VI. H. M. Queen Elizabeth the Queen Mother and H. M. Queen Mary.* [c. 1953]

A pop-up book. Pictures by 'Dinah'. Price 2/-.

218 NURSERY RHYMES. [*Dean's Rag Book Co. Ltd., 61 High Path, London S.W.19.* c. 1955. Price 3d.]

219 NURSERY RHYME CROSSWORD BOOK. [*Birn Brothers Ltd.* c. 1955]

220 NURSERY RHYMES. [Illustrated by Cicely Steed. A Little Hercules book printed in Great Britain by Thomas Nelson and Sons Ltd. 1958]

Printed on paper-covered boards, and sturdily bound: it is apparently felt a little Hercules would be needed to destroy it. Price 2/6.

221 NURSERY RHYMES TRACING AND COLOURING BOOK. *Bairns Books Limited, London.* [c. 1958. Price 3d.]

222 NURSERY RHYMES. Illustrated by Lorna Steele. *Purnell and Sons, Ltd., Paulton (Somerset) and London.* 1959

Price 1/-.

223 OUR NURSERY RHYMES. [Illustrated by Cicely Steed. A Sturdibook, printed in Great Britain by Thomas Nelson and Sons Ltd. 1959]

Price 1/6.

224 LITTLE POPPET'S RHYME BOOK. Illustrated by Leslie Ellis. *Dean & Son Ltd. 41/43 Ludgate Hill, London E.C.4.* 1960

225 NURSERY RHYMES PICTURE BOOK. [*Amex Company Ltd., London.* c. 1960 Price 6d.]

226 NURSERY RHYMES TRACING & PAINTING BOOK. [*Mellifont Press Limited, 1 Furnival Street, London, E.C.4.* c. 1960. Price 6d.]

227 COUNTING RHYMES. Pictures by Sharon Kane. *Golden Pleasure Books, London.* [1962]

Apparently a version of no. 200.

228 NURSERY RHYME DOLL DRESSING and Story Book. [*Purnell.* 1963]

229 PAT-A-CAKE AND OTHER HAPPY STORIES. [*Bendix Publishing Co., Ltd., London.* c. 1963]

A shaped book with pictures by F. Woof. Purchased in Woolworths, January 1964. Price 1/-.

230 NURSERY RHYMES. [*Murrays Sales & Service Co., 63 St. Pauls Road, London N.1.* c. 1964]

A sixpenny picture book giving simply the titles of the rhymes, the texts apparently being thought unnecessary.

231 MY NEW NURSERY RHYME BOOK. [*Murrays Sales & Service Co., 63 St. Pauls Road, London, N.1.* c. 1964]

Same series as above.

232 NURSERY RHYMES. [Printed in Holland. Brown Watson Ltd., London. c. 1964]

A booklet similar to the above, with a different illustrator.

233 NURSERY RHYMES PAINTING BOOK. [*Sandle's, London, W.14.* c. 1964]

234 NURSERY RHYMES. Illustrations by Mabette Jardine. [*Sandle's, London W.14.* 1967. Price 1/-]

235 NURSERY RHYME BOOK. [*Sandle's, London W.14.* c. 1972]

8 pp. printed on card in Holland. Price 5p.

4 Illustrious Illustrators

In this section most of the artists are not so much illustrating nursery rhymes, as using nursery rhymes as a vehicle for their talent. Such artists as Byam Shaw, Lovat Fraser, Mervyn Peake, and Charles Addams, could easily not have had children in mind while they worked; and Alexander Calder certainly did not. Kate Greenaway, on the other hand, probably thought she was illustrating for children, and has always most pleased the middle-aged. The gusto of John Hassall now appeals to the newly mature who can enjoy few contemporary illustrators possessing his certainty about life. Willebeek Le Mair's gentle pictures continue to be held in affection by those who were brought up on them. Walter Crane has risen again in esteem on the high tide of Art Nouveau. And Arthur Rackham is unique in never having fallen out of fashion. But if we are looking for an artist whom grandparent and grandchild can enjoy together, both moved by the same emotions, was ever there anyone to compare with Randolph Caldecott?

J. C. Horsley and others

236 Traditional Nursery Songs of England. With Pictures by Eminent Modern Artists. The Home Treasury. Edited by Felix Summerly. *London: Joseph Cundall, 12, Old Bond Street.* 1843

The first nursery rhyme book to be illustrated by artists of repute. 'Felix Summerly' was the name adopted for business purposes by Henry Cole, later Sir Henry Cole. A man of wide acquaintance, the artists he induced to illustrate this volume were J. C. Horsley, Richard Redgrave, John Linell, C. W. Cope, and Thomas Webster. The volume, with its good print and hand-coloured illustrations, was one that helped set a new standard in the production of books for the young.

237 Nursery Rhymes, Tales, and Jingles. *London. Frederick Warne and Co.* [c. 1870]

First published 1844. This was one of the first nursery rhyme books to be affected by the high-class production of 'The Home Treasury', above. This edition includes designs by Horsley and Cope, while others may be by William Dyce.

Thomas Webster

238 Gammer Gurton's Garland. *Joseph Cundall, 12, Old Bond Street.* [c. 1845]

Gammer Gurton's Story Books, no. 3, edited by W. J. Thoms. The hand-coloured frontispiece of this 16 pp. booklet is the picture Webster did of Mother Hubbard for 'The Home Treasury', here re-engraved by W. G. and G. E. Mason.

239 Gammer Gurton's Garland. With an illustration by T. Webster, R.A. *Chapman and Hall, London.* [c. 1855]

This edition also has sixteen pages, but a larger selection of rhymes. The frontispiece is uncoloured.

John Absolon, Harrison Weir, and others

240 A Treasury of Pleasure Books for Young Children. With more than One Hundred Illustrations by John Absolon and Harrison Weir. *London: Grant and Griffith, Successors to Newbery and Harris, St. Paul's Churchyard; and Joseph Cundall, Old Bond Street.* 1850

Twenty-one nursery booklets, with titles such as 'The Simple Story of Simple Simon' and 'The Wonderful History of Mother Goose', brought together in one volume with a preface signed 'J.C.' (Joseph Cundall). This publication is a further one to have benefitted by the example of 'The Home Treasury' (no. 236).

241 A Treasury of Pleasure Books for Young People. Illustrated with One Hundred and Forty Pictures by eminent Artists. *London: Addey and Co. Henrietta Street, Covent Garden.* [c. 1855]

A later edition, with hand-coloured engravings. The contents of the booklets has been rearranged, and six more stories have been added, some of them illustrated by Kenny Meadows and Edward Wehnert.

See also nos. 102, 104, 482.

Eleanor Vere Boyle

242 Child's Play. Seventeen Drawings by E. V. B. Second Edition. *London: Addey and Co., 21 Old Bond Street.* 1853

First published 1852. A collection of sixteen rhymes arranged one to a page with its illustration. A drawingroom book rather than a nursery book.

243 Child's Play. By E. V. B. *London: Sampson Low, Son & Co. 47, Ludgate Hill.* 1859

Fifteen nursery rhymes, each illustrated with a full-page coloured lithograph on the opposite page. The title-page is hand-coloured.

244 Child's Play. E. V. B. *London: Sampson Low, Marston, Searle, & Rivington.* 1881

Some of the pictures are from *Child's Play*, above, and some from *New Child's Play*, 1877. 'By a wonderful process of electrotyping,' explains the artist, 'they have all been reduced to a much smaller size'.

Charles H. Bennett

245 Old Nurse's Book of Rhymes, Jingles and Ditties. Edited and Illustrated by Charles H. Bennett, Author of "Shadows," etc. With Ninety Engravings. *London: Griffith and Farran, (Late Grant and Griffith, successors to Newbery and Harris) Corner of St. Paul's Churchyard.* 1858

C. H. Bennett was perhaps the first man to enter into the spirit of the nursery rhymes, and to laugh wholeheartedly with his young public at the world's absurdity.

See also no. 386.

Henry Stacey Marks

246 Nursery Rhymes. *George Routledge & Sons, Broadway, Ludgate Hill.* [1865]

Routledge's Shilling Toy Books, no. 1.

247 Nursery Rhymes. With Pictures by H. S. Marks, A.R.A. *George Routledge & Sons.* [1871 ?]

Routledge's Shilling Toy Books, no. 1. The quality of the colour plates in this later edition has much deteriorated.

248 Nursery Songs. *London: George Routledge & Sons, Broadway, Ludgate Hill.* [1865]

Routledge's Shilling Toy Books, no. 9.

Sir John Millais

249 Little Songs for me to Sing. The Illustrations by J. E. Millais, R.A. (Engraved by Joseph Swain). With Music Composed by Henry Leslie. *London: Cassell Petter & Galpin.* [1865].

Dedicated to Her Royal Highness The Princess of Wales. Six songs, including "Twinkle, twinkle, little star" and "Mary's Little Lamb".

250 Leslie's Songs for Little Folks. By Henry Leslie. With Eight Original Illustrations by Sir J. E. Millais, Bart., R.A. Price Two Shillings. *London: J. B. Cramer & Co., 201, Regent Street, W.* [1873]

An enlarged edition of *Little Songs for me to Sing*.

Keeley Halswelle

251 The Illustrated Book of Nursery Rhymes and Songs. With Music. Edited by T. L. Hately. Illustrations by Keeley Halswelle. *T. Nelson and Sons: London, Edinburgh and New York.* [1865]

252 The Illustrated Book of Nursery Rhymes and Songs. With Music. Illustrations by Keeley Halswelle. *London: T. Nelson and Sons, Paternoster Row. Edinburgh; and New York.* 1882

A reissue, with glossy pictorial cover. The size of the illustrations has been reduced, and they are printed on tinted backgrounds.

Alfred Crowquill

253 Nursery Rhymes (Nos. 2 and 3) Illustrated by Alfred Crowquill. *T. Nelson & Sons, London & Edinburgh.* [c. 1865]

'Alfred Crowquill' was the caricaturist A. H. Forrester.

Marcus Ward

254 The Royal Illuminated Book of Nursery Rhymes. The Old Familiar Words. Set to appropriate Music; arranged in an easy style suited to little Minstrels. Each Story is illustrated by Pictures, designed in the quaint spirit of Mediaeval times, and printed in Colors and Gold, By Marcus Ward, Illuminator to The Queen. First Series. [Second Series.] *Edinburgh: William P. Nimmo.* [1872]

Both volumes contain four sections, which had been issued separately each with four plates.

Walter Crane

255 1. 2. Buckle my Shoe. *London: George Routledge & Sons.* [1867]

No. 78 in Routledge's New Sixpenny Toy Books.

256 The Fairy Ship. *London: George Routledge & Sons.* [1869]

No. 95 in Routledge's New Sixpenny Toy Books. The volume illustrates 'I saw a ship a-sailing' (*ODNR* no. 470).

257 Grammar in Rhyme. *London: George Routledge & Sons.* [1872]

No. 70 in Routledge's New Sixpenny Toy Books. Illustrates the mnemonic 'Three little words you often see'.

258 The Absurd A.B.C. Walter Crane's Toy Books New Series. *George Routledge & Sons.* [c. 1873]

No. 110 in Routledge's New Sixpenny Toy Books.

259 Baby's Own Alphabet. Walter Crane's Toy Books New Series. *George Routledge & Sons.* [1874]

No. 114 in Routledge's New Sixpenny Toy Books. *ODNR* plate 1.

260 The Alphabet of Old Friends. Walter Crane's Toy Books Shilling Series. *London and New York: George Routledge and Sons.* [1875]

No. 73 in Routledge's Shilling Toy Books.

261 The Baby's Opera. A Book of Old Rhymes with New Dresses by Walter Crane, Engraved, & Printed in Colours by Edmund Evans. The Music by the Earliest Masters. *London & New York. George Routledge and Sons.* [1877]

Walter Crane later recalled that 'The Trade' was doubtful whether a book could succeed which cost five shillings, and was not bound in cloth and gilt-stamped. In fact its success was immediate; and it started a fashion for pictorial boards.

262 The Baby's Bouquet: A Fresh Bunch of Old Rhymes & Tunes. A Companion to the "Baby's Opera". The Tunes Collected and Arranged by L. C. Arranged & Decorated by Walter Crane. Cut & Printed in Colours by Edmund Evans. *London: Frederick Warne & Co., Ltd. and New York.* [1878]

This collection included French and German songs as well as British. As with the *Baby's Opera* the tunes were arranged by Crane's sister Lucy.

See also nos. 382, 456, 536, 549, 551.

Randolph Caldecott

263 The Diverting History of John Gilpin. One of R. Caldecott's Picture Books. *George Routledge & Sons.* One Shilling. [1878]

The first impression, with the blue card covers. Shown with a letter from Caldecott to William Allingham, 7 June 1878, written when he was about to 'arrange in the seclusion of rustic retirement the illustrations of a well-known "diverting history".'

264 An Elegy on the Death of a Mad Dog. Written by Dr. Goldsmith. Pictured by R. Caldecott. Sung By Master Bill Primrose. [One of R. Caldecott's Picture Books. *George Routledge and Sons.* 1879]

265 The Babes in the Wood. One of R. Caldecott's Picture Books. *George Routledge & Sons.* [1879]

266 The Three Jovial Huntsmen. One of R. Caldecott's Picture Books. *George Routledge & Sons.* [1880]

267 The Farmer's Boy. One of R. Caldecott's Picture Books. *Geo. Routledge & Sons.* [1881]

268 Hey Diddle Diddle and Baby Bunting. R. Caldecott's Picture Books. *George Routledge & Sons.* One Shilling. [1882]

Caldecott's six original paintings for this book, executed on proofs of the sepia key-blocks, are also on view.

269 The Fox jumps over the Parson's Gate. R. Caldecott's Picture Books. *George Routledge & Sons.* Price One Shilling. [1883]

270 Come Lasses and Lads. R. Caldecott's Picture Books. *George Routledge & Sons London.* Price One Shilling. [1884]

271 Ride A-Cock Horse to Banbury ✠ & A Farmer Went Trotting Upon His Grey Mare. R. Caldecott's Picture Books. *George Routledge & Sons.* [1884]

272 An Elegy on the Glory of her Sex Mrs Mary Blaize. R. Caldecott's Picture Books. *George Routledge & Sons.* Price One Shilling. [1885]

273 The Great Panjandrum Himself. R. Caldecott's Picture Books. *George Routledge & Sons.* Price One Shilling. [1885]

274 The Complete Collection of Pictures & Songs by Randolph Caldecott. Engraved and Printed by Edmund Evans. With a Preface by Austin Dobson. *London: George Routledge and Sons, Broadway, Ludgate Hill. Glasgow, and New York.* 1887.

This volume reproduces all sixteen of Caldecott's

29

shilling Picture Books, together with their covers. Large paper edition limited to 800 copies. Signed by Edmund Evans.

275 Randolph Caldecott's Painting Book. *Society for Promoting Christian Knowledge. London: Northumberland Avenue, W.C.; 43 Queen Victoria Street, E.C. Brighton: 129 North Street. New York: E. & J. B. Young & Co.* Price One Shilling. [1895]

Contains pictures for children to colour, selected from *The House that Jack Built, The Three Jovial Huntsmen*, and others of Caldecott's Picture Books.

276 Set of 48 postcards, numbered A1 to H6, reproducing four pictures from each of twelve of Caldecott's shilling Picture Books. *F. Warne & Co.* [c. 1925]

See also nos. 389, 457, 464, 477.

Kate Greenaway

277 Mother Goose or the Old Nursery Rhymes. Illustrated by Kate Greenaway, engraved and printed by Edmund Evans. *London and New York: George Routledge and Sons.* [1881].

The little volume is in its original printed dust jacket.

See also nos. 606, 773.

Alice B. Woodward

278 Banbury Cross & Other Nursery Rhymes. Illustrated by Alice B. Woodward. *London: Published by J. M. Dent & Co at Aldine House in Great Eastern Street.* 1895.

One of the Banbury Cross Series.

Paul Woodroffe

279 Ye Second Booke of Nursery Rhymes. Set to Music by Joseph Moorat & Pictured by Paul Woodroffe. *George Allen, Ruskin House, Charing ✠ Rd, London.* [1896]

The first book was published in 1895.

280 Thirty Old-Time Nursery Songs Arranged by Joseph Moorat & Pictured by Paul Woodroffe. *London: T. C. & E. C. Jack. New York: Frederick A. Stokes Co.* [1907]

281 Humpty Dumpty & Other Songs. By Joseph Moorat & Pictured by Paul Woodroffe. *Oxford. Basil Blackwell, Broad Street.* 1920

L. Leslie Brooke

282 The Nursery Rhyme Book. Edited by Andrew Lang. Illustrated by L. Leslie Brooke. *London: Frederick Warne and Co: and New York.* 1897.

283 The Man in the Moon. A Nursery Rhyme Picture Book. With Drawings by L. Leslie Brooke. *Frederick Warne & Co., Ltd. London and New York.* [1913]

One of 'Leslie Brooke's Little Books', as are the next three titles.

284 Oranges and Lemons. A Nursery Rhyme Picture Book. With Drawings by L. Leslie Brooke. *Frederick Warne & Co., Ltd. London and New York.* [1913]

285 This Little Pig Went to Market. A Nursery Rhyme Picture Book. With Drawings by L. Leslie Brooke. *Frederick Warne & Co., Ltd. London and New York.* [1922]

286 Little Bo-Peep. A Nursery Rhyme Picture Book. With Drawings by L. Leslie Brooke. *Frederick Warne & Co., Ltd., London and New York.* [1922]

Cecil Aldin

287 The Young Folks Birthday Book. Nursery Rhymes, Illustrated with Coloured Pictures by Cecil Aldin. *London: Printed and Published by Hills & Co., Ltd., 2, Bayer Street, Golden Lane, E.C.* [1898]

See also nos. 591–2.

Byam Shaw

288 Old King Cole's book of Nursery Rhymes. *Macmillan and Co., Limited, London. New York: The Macmillan Company.* [1901]

The illustrations are unashamedly adult, and have both strength and sumptuousness. The artist has inscribed this copy 'drorn by Byam Shaw'.

John Hassall

289 Mother Goose's Nursery Rhymes. Edited by Walter Jerrold. Illustrated by John Hassall R.I. *Blackie & Son Limited: London Glasgow Dublin Bombay.* 1909

Hassall family copy, the gift of Miss Joan Hassall, with emendations in John Hassall's hand.

290 Mother Goose Nursery Rhymes. From Designs by John Hassall. No. 141 Dean's Rag Books, Patented. *London: Dean's Rag Book Co. Ltd.* [c. 1910]

The gift of Miss Joan Hassall.

291 Hey! Diddle Diddle & Other Nursery Rhymes. Blackie's New Picture Books. [c. 1920]

With illustrations, including cover, by John Hassall. The gift of Miss Joan Hassall.

292 Mother Goose's Book of Nursery Stories Rhymes and Fables. *Blackie & Son Limited: London and Glasgow.* [1928]

Illustrated by John Hassall, Charles Robinson, and others. The magnificent cover is by John Hassall. The gift of Miss Joan Hassall.

293 The Good Old Nursery Rhymes. Illustrated by John Hassall. *Blackie and Son Limited, London, Glasgow, Dublin, Bombay, New York.* [c. 1930]

Coloured illustrations throughout, some of them the same as in *Mother Goose's Nursery Rhymes,* 1909.

See also nos. 591–2, 692, 694, 695, 698.

H. Willebeek Le Mair

294 Our Old Nursery Rhymes. The original tunes harmonized by Alfred Moffat. Illustrated by H. Willebeek Le Mair. *Augener Ltd. London.*

First published 1911. This is a later printing. Also shown is a shilling packet containing 12 postcard reproductions of pictures in the book.

295 Little Songs of Long Ago: "More old Nursery Rhymes". The original tunes harmonized by Alfred Moffat. Illustrated by H. Willebeek Le Mair. *Augener Ltd. London. For the Book Trade A. & C. Black, London. G. Schirmer, New-York.* [1912].

Also shown is a shilling packet containing 12 postcard reproductions of pictures in the book.

296 What the Children Sing. A Book of The Most Popular Nursery Songs, Rhymes & Games. With the Traditional Tunes harmonised by Alfred Moffat. Cover design by H. Willebeek Le Mair. *Augener Ltd. 18 Great Marlborough Street, 63 Conduit Street (Regent Street Corner) & 57 High Street, Marylebone, London, W.1.* [1915]

297 Grannie's Little Rhyme Book. No. 1 of Old Nursery Rhymes. Illustrated by H. Willebeek Le Mair. *Augener Ltd. 63 Conduit Street, London, W.* [c. 1915]

Selection of rhymes and pictures from the larger volumes of 1911 and 1912. No tunes.

298 Auntie's Little Rhyme Book. No. 3 of Old Nursery Rhymes. Illustrated by H. Willebeek Le Mair. *Augener Ltd. London. David McKay, 604–608 South Washington Square, Philadelphia* [c. 1915]

Arthur Rackham

299 Mother Goose, The Old Nursery Rhymes. Illustrated by Arthur Rackham. *London: William Heinemann.* [1913]

An exquisite book, which adult and child can appreciate together, each in his own way; but not perhaps a book the child would want to look at when on his own.

Claud Lovat Fraser

300 Nurse Lovechild's Legacy, Being a Mighty Fine Collection of the Most Noble, Memorable and Veracious Nursery Rhymes. Now first embellished by C. L. F. for the Poetry Bookshop. *Printed for The Poetry Bookshop, 35 Devonshire Street, Theobalds Road, London W.C.* 1916. One Shilling & Sixpence Net.

The illustrations were inspired by the woodcuts heading the early nineteenth century broadsides and slip sheets. A copy dated 1919, 'Third Thousand,' is also possessed, price one shilling; and one dated 1922, 'Sixth Thousand,' which is in larger format, price half a crown.

301 Nursery Rhymes with pictures by C. Lovat Fraser. *London, T. C. & E. C. Jack, Lim: 35 Paternoster Row E.C.* [1919]

The bold and highly effective use of colour obscures, at first glance, the sublety of the humour in the drawings, a subtlety that is more likely to be appreciated by adults than by children.

Lawson Wood

302 The Lawson Wood Nursery Rhyme Book. *Nelson.* [c. 1930.]

Charles Folkard

303 The Land of Nursery Rhyme, As Seen by Alice Daglish and Ernest Rhys. With a Map and Pictures Drawn by Charles Folkard. *London: J. M. Dent & Sons Ltd. New York: E. P. Dutton & Co.* [1946]

First published in 1932.

Mervyn Peake

304 Ride a Cock-Horse And Other Nursery Rhymes. Illustrated by Mervyn Peake. *Chatto and Windus: London.* 1940

The other-worldliness of the nursery rhymes, and the human predicament of the nursery rhyme characters, is precisely conveyed in this most elegantly-designed of nursery rhyme books. Two copies are shown so that the book can be fully appreciated.

c

Alexander Calder

305 Three Young Rats and Other Rhymes. Drawings by Alexander Calder. Edited with Introduction by James Johnson Sweeney. *The Museum of Modern Art: New York* [1946].

First published 1944. A distinguished abstract sculptor illustrates nursery rhymes in a most unabstract manner.

Joan Hassall

306 Scottish Children's Rhymes and Lullabies. Designed by Joan Hassall. Saltire Chapbook No. 9. 1948. Price 1/-.

The Saltire Society's series of chapbooks, printed by R. & R. Clark, Ltd., Edinburgh, during the 1940s, can be considered the culmination of chapbook publishing. It is difficult to imagine small booklets of traditional matter that could be more lovely; and the particular circumstances which arose during the war, when midget booklets could achieve commercial success, are perhaps unlikely to reoccur.

307 The Fause Knight and other Fancies. Chosen by J. M. Reid. Designed by Joan Hassall. Saltire Chapbook No. 10. 1950. Price 1/-.

See also nos. 61, 811.

Maurice Sendak

308 Lullabies and Night Songs. Music by Alec Wilder. Edited by William Engvick. *Harper & Row, Publishers. New York.* [1965]

Sendak is one of the few contemporary illustrators who uses his own terms of reference, but whose world is instantly recognisable as belonging to our own past. Presentation copy, prompted by Mr Justin Schiller, embellished with a portrait of a Wild Thing.

Charles Addams

309 The Chas Addams Mother Goose. *Collins: St James's Place, London,* 1967

A bold attempt to disregard the conventional settings, and see nursery rhymes anew. The book may disturb the squeamish; but the difference between the work of Charles Addams and the pictures in the horror comics is clear enough: Charles Addams is funny.

5 Celebrated Characters

This section brings together picture books and booklets which feature a single nursery rhyme story. In oral tradition the characters they celebrate often have wonderfully brief histories; but here the short rhymes are arbitrarily extended, usually to fourteen or fifteen verses, to meet the requirements of the sixteen-page copperplate books and chapbooks. It was to this end Sarah Catherine Martin added verses to Old Mother Hubbard to make the total fourteen, and Charles Lamb painfully spun out the tale of the King and Queen of Hearts to fill a like number of pages. And it was probably due as much to their convenient length, as to their popularity, that 'My Mother' and 'The Butterfly's Ball' obtained entry to the chapbook series (nos. 735–737 and 748–753). The circulation these verse-tales have achieved can be gauged from the fact that shown here are twenty-two editions of 'The House that Jack Built', thirty-three editions of 'Old Mother Hubbard', and fifty-two editions of Cock Robin with or without Jenny Wren. Even so insignificant a character as Dame Trot, who fell out of favour about a hundred years ago, is represented with fifteen editions; while to the twenty-two straight editions of 'The House that Jack Built' can be added the seven individually-published parodies and imitations. (Parodies and imitations, if any, follow immediately after the main entries for each character.) Further, we are inevitably showing here only a fraction of the editions actually published. After being able to show a first edition of Mother Hubbard, published by Harris in 1805, we count ourselves fortunate in possessing even the twenty-fourth edition, issued two years later.

Cock Robin and Jenny Wren

310 The Death and Burial of Cock Robin: as Taken from the original Manuscript, in the Possession of Master Meanwell. *Lichfield: Printed and Sold by M. Morgan, and A. Morgan, Stafford.* [c. 1797]

The chapbook is displayed with a second copy, unfolded to show how the sixteen pages are made from a single sheet.

311 The Death & Burial of Cock Robin. Price 6d. Coloured. *Publish'd by G. Martin, 6, Great St. Thomas Apostle.* [c. 1810]

Engraved throughout, with hand-coloured illustrations.

312 The Death and Burial of Cock Robin. Illustrated with Sixteen Copper-plate Engravings. *London: Printed for the Booksellers* [by Charles Squire, Printer, Furnival's-Inn-Court, London]. Price 1s. Plain, or 1s. 6d. Coloured. [1813 ?]

A coloured copy. The frontispiece has the imprint 'Published by W. Darton Junr 58 Holborn Hill, Jany 31st 1806'.

313 Cock Robin. A Pretty Painted Toy for Either Girl or Boy; Suited to Children of All Ages. *London: Printed for J. Harris and Son, Corner of St. Paul's Church-yard.* 1819.

Publisher's specimen pages of the third title in Harris's Cabinet of Amusement & Instruction.

314 Cock Robin. A Pretty Painted Toy . . . *London: John Harris, Corner of St. Paul's Church-yard.* [c. 1825]

315 The Life and Death of Cock Robin. Adorn'd with Colour'd Plates. *London: Published by J. Bysh, 52, Paternoster Row.* [c. 1820]

Text and illustrations engraved throughout.

316 The Courtship, Marriage, and Pic Nic Dinner of Cock Robin and Jenny Wren. *York: Printed by J. Kendrew, Colliergate, York.* [c. 1820]

The Life and Death of

JENNY WREN

FOR THE USE OF

YOUNG LADIES AND GENTLEMEN

Being

A very small Book,
At a very small charge,
To learn them to read,
Before they grow large

Printed by **J. CATNACH,**
2, Monmouth-Court, 7 Dials

317 The Life and Death of Jenny Wren for the Use of Young Ladies and Gentlemen. Being
A very small Book,
At a very small charge,
To learn them to read,
Before they grow large.
Printed by J. Catnach, 2, Monmouth Court, 7 Dials. [c. 1820]

318 The Life and Death of Jenny Wren. *York: Printed by J. Kendrew, Colliergate.* [c. 1820]

319 An Elegy on the Death and Burial of Cock Robin. Ornamented with Cuts. *York: Printed by J. Kendrew, 23, Colliergate.* [c. 1820]

320 The Courtship, Merry Marriage, and Pic-nic Dinner, of Cock Robin and Jenny Wren. To which is added, Alas! The Doleful Death of the Bridegroom. *London: Printed for J. Harris and Son, Corner of St. Paul's Church-yard.* 1822.

Harris's Cabinet of Amusement and Instruction.

321 The Tragical History of the Death and Burial of Cock Robin. Embellished with Coloured Engravings. *London: Printed and Sold by E. Marshall, 140, Fleet Street.* Price One Shilling. [c. 1823]

Engraved throughout, and gaudily hand-coloured in the Marshall style.

322 The Death and Burial of Cock Robin. Embellished with Superior Coloured Engravings. *London: Printed and Sold by J. Innes, 61, Wells Street, Oxford Street.* Price Sixpence. [c. 1828]

323 The Courtship, Marriage and Pic-nic Dinner, of Cock Robin and Jenny Wren: with the Death and Burial of Poor Cock Robin. Embellished with Sixteen Neatly-coloured Engravings. *London: Dean and Munday, Threadneedle-Street; and A. K. Newman & Co. Leadenhall-Street.* Price Six-pence. [c. 1830]

324 The Courtship, Marriage, and Pic-nic Dinner, of Cock Robin and Jenny Wren . . . *London: A. K. Newman & Co. Leadenhall-Street.* Price Six-pence. [c. 1830]

As above, with alternative imprint.

325 The Courtship, Marriage, and Pic-nic Dinner of Cock Robin and Jenny Wren. *London: Hodgson's Wholesale Book and Print Warehouse, 111 Fleet Street.* [c. 1830]

326 Cock Robin's Alphabet. *Fairburn's Edition.* [c. 1830]

Printed by Fairburn, 110 Minories.

327 Death and Burial of Cock Robin. *Banbury: Printed by J. G. Rusher.* [c. 1840]

328 History of Jenny Wren. *London: Printed for the Booksellers.* [c. 1840]

As with the other titles in this series of chapbooks the illustrations are hand-coloured on four of the eight pages.

329 The Death and Burial of Cock Robin: To which is added The Natural History of that Bird. *London: Richardson and Son, 172, Fleet St.; 9, Capel Street, Dublin; and Derby. Price One Penny.* [c. 1840]

330 The Death and Burial of Cock Robin. *Printed by W. S. Johnson, 60, St. Martin's Lane.* [c. 1845]

Cover picture shows children mourning a robin that is as big as a turkey.

331 Aunt Affable's Story about Cock Robin Alive and Well Again. *London: Dean & Co., Threadneedle St.* [c. 1845]

A rewriting of the tale, in which the accidental shooting of Cock Robin does not prove fatal.

332 The Life and Death of Jenny Wren. *James Paul and Co., Printers, 2 & 3, Monmouth Court, Seven Dials.* [c. 1845]

333 Death & Burial of Cock Robin. *Printed for the Booksellers. [Otley: Yorkshire J. S. Publishing & Stationery Co., Limited.* c. 1850]

334 Cock Robin and Jenny Wren. *Printed for the Booksellers. [Otley: Yorkshire J. S. Publishing & Stationery Co., Limited.* c. 1850]

335 The Story of the Life and Death of Jenny Wren. With the Story of The Fox and the Farmer. Illustrated with Eight Pictures by Harrison Weir. *London: Sampson Low, Son, & Co., 47 Ludgate Hill.*

First published 1853.

336 Little Cock Robin Pictorial Quadrilles by Charles D'Albert. *London, Chappell, 50 New Bond Street, Paris Brandus.* [1854]

337 The Owl's Party,—Cock Robin,—and other Pictures. The Children's Plain and Painted Picture Book, no. 9. *London, Dean & Son, Ludgate Hill, E.C.* [1860]

Gold embossed paper cover. Each opening consists of two identical pages, one coloured and the other plain for the child to colour. The Owl's Party, to which Cock Robin is invited, is an imitation of 'The Butterfly's Ball', and appears together with a version of 'Who killed Cock Robin?'.

338 The Death and Burial of Cock Robin. *William S. Fortey, 2 & 3, Monmouth Court, Seven Dials, London.* [c. 1860]

339 Cock Robin: A Pretty Painted Toy for Either Girl or Boy; Suited to Children of All Ages. *London: Griffith and Farran, Successors to Newbery & Harris, Corner of St. Paul's Churchyard.* [c. 1860]

Mounted on linen. A late issue of no. 313 published in 1819.

340 Poor Cock Robin. *W. Walker & Sons, Otley.* [c. 1860]

A single sheet, 5 × 15 ins, folded to make eight pages.

341 Park's Cock Robin. *London: Pub. by A. Park, 47, Leonard Street.* [c. 1860]

The hand-colouring is crude compared with Park's earlier publications.

342 The Death and Burial of Cock Robin. *London: Ward & Lock, 158, Fleet Street.* [c. 1860]

Aunt Affable's Pretty Play-Books series. This copy is the Indestructible Edition, printed on specially prepared strong linen, and hand-coloured. Price one shilling.

343 Death and Burial of Poor Cock Robin. House that Jack Built. Dean's Untearable Children's Colored Story Books. *London: Dean & Son, Juvenile and Educational Book Publishers, 11, Ludgate Hill.* [1863]

The pages are mounted on linen.

344 The Death and Burial of Cock Robin. *T. Nelson & Sons, London & Edinburgh.* [c. 1865]

345 Cock Robin. One of the parts in *Aunt Friendly's Gift* [1867]. See no. 109.

Also issued separately. The illustrations of this part are by Walter Crane. The cover design, signed W. H., is different from no. 109.

346 Cock Robin. *London: Ward, Lock & Tyler, Warwick House, Paternoster Row.* [c. 1870]

A Warwick House Toy Book 'Price 1s. Beautifully Colored'.

347 The Courtship, Marriage, Death and Burial of Cock Robin. Original Illustrations by Henry Stannard. *London, Frederick Warne & Co.* [c. 1870]

Aunt Louisa's London Toy Books, no. 31. Illustrated by Henry Stannard.

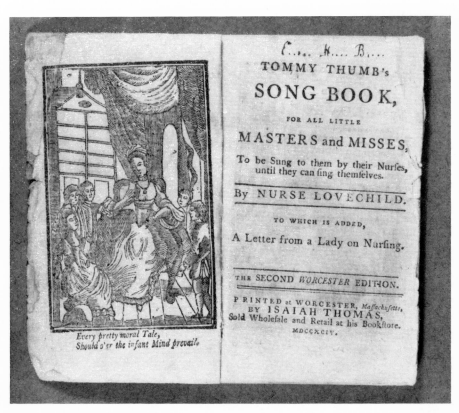

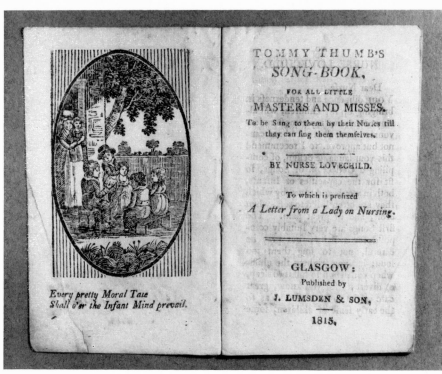

16 and 17. Two editions of *Tommy Thumb's Song Book*, believed to be reprints of the first nursery rhyme book, issued in 1744. One was printed at Worcester, Massachusetts, in 1794; the other in Glasgow, 1815.

33. 'Baa baa, black sheep' in *Songs for the Nursery*, 1822.

508. The 'hosier' plate, in *The Comic Adventures of Old Mother Hubbard*, 1805, in its first state, with a chair seemingly being levitated, and no picture on the wall.

462. The Queen of Hearts being given smelling salts on discovering the loss of her tarts. Depicted by Percy Cruikshank.

405. 'The Cow and Maid' in Webb, Millington & Co's *The House that Jack Built*, 1849.

138. The cover of Dean's *Nursery Rhymes ABC*, c. 1890. 12¼ × 9⅘ ins.

Within the illustration:
GOOSEY GOOSEY GANDER
BYAM SHAW
...STAIRS & DOWNSTAIRS & IN MY LADY'S CHAMBER

288. 'Goosey Goosey Gander' depicted by Byam Shaw, 1901.

680. An advertising showcard, c. 1890.

§10. A picture postcard sent to a young lady on holiday at Ramsgate, 5 August 1911.

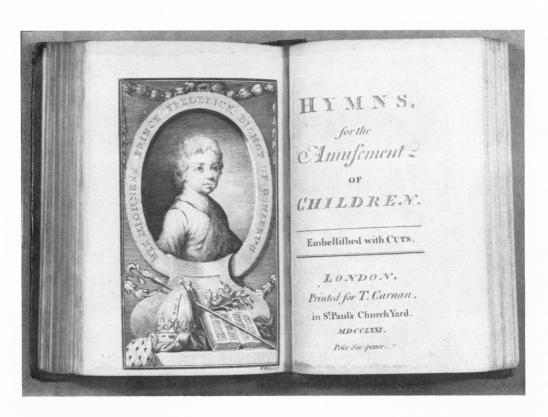

724 and 721. Christopher Smart as children's poet. *Hymns for the Amusement of Children*, 1771, published at the end of his life; and, twenty years earlier, *The Lilliputian Magazine*, to which he was a contributor.

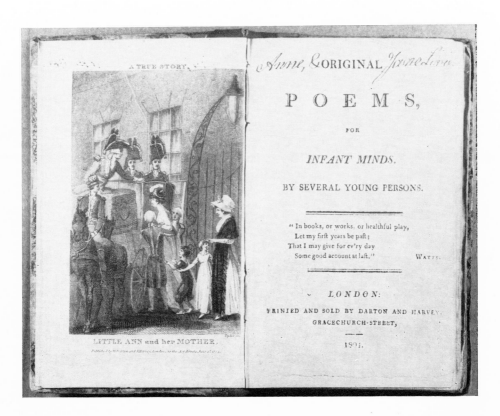

A TRUE STORY.

Anne, &c ORIGINAL Jane Lane

P O E M S,

FOR

INFANT MINDS.

BY SEVERAL YOUNG PERSONS.

" In books, or works, or healthful play,
Let my first years be past;
That I may give for ev'ry day
Some good account at last."   WATTS.

LONDON:
PRINTED AND SOLD BY DARTON AND HARVEY,
GRACECHURCH-STREET,

1804.

LITTLE ANN and her MOTHER.

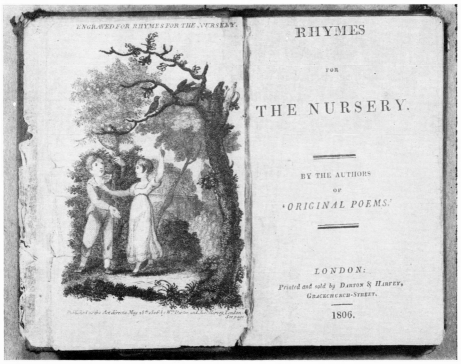

ENGRAVED FOR RHYMES FOR THE NURSERY.

RHYMES

FOR

THE NURSERY.

BY THE AUTHORS
OF
'ORIGINAL POEMS.'

LONDON:
Printed and sold by DARTON & HARVEY,
GRACECHURCH-STREET.

1806.

731 and 742. The two books which introduced the poetry of Ann and Jane Taylor: *Original Poems for Infant Minds*, 1804, and *Rhymes for the Nursery*, 1806.

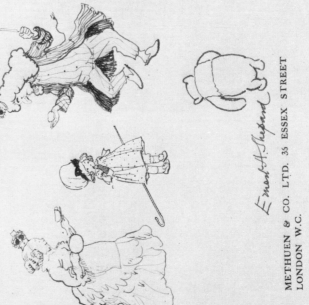

WHEN WE WERE
VERY YOUNG BY
A. A. MILNE WITH
DECORATIONS BY
ERNEST H. SHEPARD

Ernest H. Shepard

METHUEN & CO. LTD. 35 ESSEX STREET
LONDON W.C.

828. The title-page of *When We Were Very Young*, 1924,
extra-illustrated by Ernest H. Shepard. Little Bo-Peep, who
ordinarily stands alone, is here seen in distinguished company.

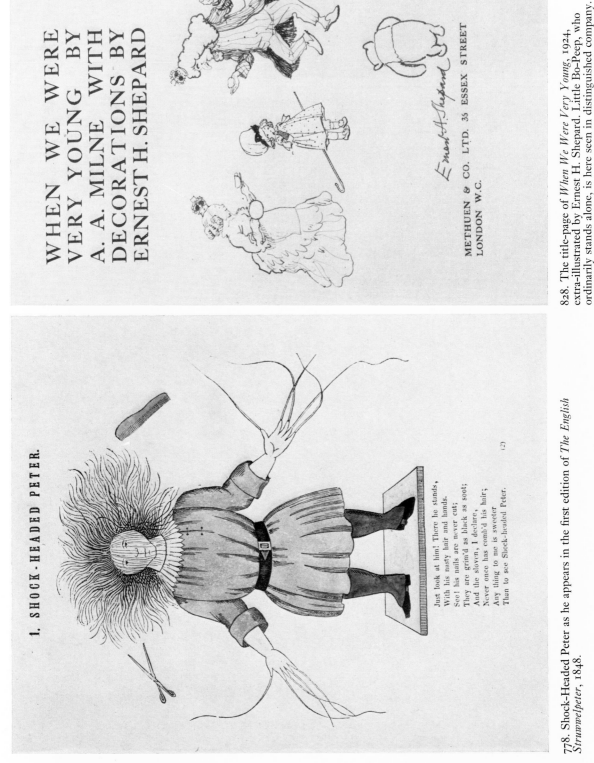

1. SHOCK-HEADED PETER.

Just look at him! There he stands,
With his nasty hair and hands.
See! his nails are never cut;
They are grim'd as black as soot;
And the sloven, I declare,
Never once has comb'd his hair;
Any thing to me is sweeter
Than to see Shock-headed Peter.

(2)

778. Shock-Headed Peter as he appears in the first edition of *The English*
Struwwelpeter, 1848.

348 Courtship & Marriage of Cock Robin. Death and Burial of Cock Robin. The House that Jack Built. Dame Trot and Her Cat. Illustrated. Price 2s. [c. 1870]

Probably the last form in which Harris's Cabinet of Amusement appeared. Four titles, uncoloured, bound together in crimson paper boards, with a plain label. The 2nd and 3rd items retain their title pages with the Griffith and Farran imprint, see no. 339.

349 The Death of Cock Robin. *London: Read, Brooks and Co., Printers and Publishers, 25 & 26, New Street, Cloth Fair, E.C.* [c. 1875]

One of Grandmama Goodsoul's Series, 'Printed in Oil Colors, on Paper and Linen'.

350 Cock Robin's Death & Burial. *London: Frederick Warne and Co.* [c. 1875]

One of Warne's Large Picture Toy Books, according to front cover, but probably no. 44 in their Excelsior Toy Books series. Mounted on linen. The portrayal of Robin's death leaves nothing to the imagination.

351 'Cock Robin With Variations and Illustrations. An Old Tale Retold. By Palmer Cox.' Contained in Queer People with Wings and Stings and their Kweer Kapers. Illustrated. By Palmer Cox. *London and Sydney: Griffith, Farran, Okeden & Welsh, Successors to Newbery & Harris.* [1889]

An idiosyncratic rendering of the traditional story:

Who killed Cock Robin, where the lilies grow?
I, said the sparrow, with my bow and arrow,
I laid him low.

352 Who Killed Cock Robin? *London: F. Warne & Co. & New York.* [c. 1890]
The New Wonder Toy Books, Series 1.

353 Who Killed Cock Robin? Dean's Artistic Series, No. 12. *London: Dean & Son, Ltd., 160a, Fleet Street, E.C.* [1894?]

354 Cock Robin. By B. O. A. *London: Dean & Son, 160A, Fleet Street, E.C.* [c. 1895]
One of 'Dean's Favorite Nursery Series'.

355 Who Killed Cock Robin. Dean's Gold Medal Series No. 16. *London: Dean & Son, 160a, Fleet Street, E.C.* [c. 1896]

A toy-book shaped to the illustration on the cover.

356 Who killed Cock Robin? Pictured by J. A. Shepherd. *London: Grant Richards, 9 Henrietta Street, Covent Garden, W.C.* [1900]

357 Cock Robin and Jenny Wren, or Who killed Cock Robin? *London: Ernest Nister, 24 St. Bride Street E.C. New York: E. P. Dutton & Co. 31 West Twenty Third Street.* [c. 1910]

A booklet shaped to the picture on the cover.

358 Who Killed Cock Robin? An Old Story Re-told in Modern Colour Photography by Paul Henning. *Methuen & Co. Ltd., London, 36, Essex Street, Strand, W.C.2.* [1945].

Rather too life-like, and death-like.

359 Who Killed Cock Robin? *B. B. Ltd.* [c. 1950]

In the tradition of earlier Cock Robins the original price of this eight page booklet will not have been more than 3d.

360 Who'll Wed Cock Robin? Words by Geoffrey Hall. With simple piano accompaniment . . . by Edith Bathurst in collaboration with Geoffrey Handley-Taylor. Copyright 1953 by Hinrichsen Edition Ltd.

A reformed version of the traditional story in accordance with the principles of 'True Aim' (see no. 662).

All the birds in the air
Fell a-singing and a-throbbing
When they heard of the love
Of dear Cock Robin.

361 The Death and Burial of Cock Robin. An old nursery rhyme with new illustrations by Richard Blomfield. *Printed at the Studio, Priory Road, Corsham, Wiltshire.* 1961

Wood engravings. Printed by hand by the engraver. A production of The Punch Press.

Dame Trot

362 Continuation of the Moving Adventures of Old Dame Trot and Her Comical Cat. Part 2nd. *London: Printed for the Booksellers* [by Charles Squire, Printer, Furnival's-Inn-Court, London. c. 1815]

Engraved throughout. Sold for '1s Plain, or 1s. 6d. Coloured'. This is a coloured copy, and has the original price 1/6 written on the front cover.

363 Old Dame Trot, and her comical Cat. *London: J. Catnach, 2, and 3 Monmouth Court, 7 Dials.* [c. 1820]

364 Old Dame Trot, and Her Comical Cat. *York: Printed by J. Kendrew, Colliergate.* [c. 1820]

A mildly uninhibited version, as may be seen.

365 The Comic Adventures of Old Dame Trot, and Her Cat: correctly printed from the Original in the Hubbardonian Library. *London: Printed for J. Harris and Son, Corner of St. Paul's Church-yard.* 1822

Harris's Cabinet of Amusement and Instruction, no. 2. First published 1820.

366 Dame Trot. *London: William Darton and Son, Holborn Hill. Price Sixpence.* [c. 1830]

367 Old Dame Trot and her Comical Cat. *London: E. Howes, 24, Holywell St., Strand.* [c. 1830]

368 Dame Trot and her Droll Cat. [*Devonport: Printed by S. & J. Keys.* c. 1835]

Advertised for sale at one half-penny.

369 The Renowned History of Dame Trot and her Cat. *Banbury: Printed for J. G. Rusher.* [c. 1840]

370 Dame Trot and Her Cat. *London: Printed for the Booksellers.* [c. 1840]

371 Old Dame Trot and her Cat. *London and Otley: Wm Walker and Son.* [c. 1845]

A title in The Illuminated Library for the Homes of Happy Childhood. A rewritten history in which the dame rather than her pet is the delinquent.

372 Old Dame Trot. *Printed for the Booksellers.* [*Otley: Yorkshire J. S. Publishing & Stationery Limited.* c. 1850]

373 Dame Trot and Her Cat. *Otley: William Walker & Sons.* [c. 1860]

Cover and alternate openings coloured.

374 Dame Trot and Her Cat. *Otley: William Walker & Sons.* [c. 1865]

The $4 \times 2\frac{1}{2}$ ins. block used in earlier smaller editions, has been given an ornamental frame so that it will serve for an $8\frac{1}{2} \times 6\frac{1}{4}$ ins. cover.

375 Dame Trot and Her Cat in Aunt Louisa's Our Favourites. *London and New York, Frederick Warne and Co.* [c. 1875]

376 Old Dame Trot's Picture Book. With Large Coloured Illustrations. *London: George Routledge and Sons, The Broadway, Ludgate. New York: 416 Broome Street.* [1878]

Four titles bound in one, the other three being 'The Babes in the Wood', 'The Prince with the Nose', and 'The Queen of Hearts'.

Dish that ran away with the Spoon

377 Aunt Louisa's Companion. Comprising Hey Diddle Diddle [and three other titles]. With Twenty-four Pages of Illustrations, Printed in Colours by Kronheim. *London: Frederick Warne and Co., Bedford Street, Covent Garden. New York: Scribner, Welford, and Co.* [c. 1870]

Hungry Fox

378 The Fox came thro' the Town, O. *Disley, Printer, 57, High Street, St. Giles, London.* [c. 1840]

A broadsheet.

379 Mister Fox. By Comus, Author of 'Three Little Kittens' [R. M. Ballantyne]. *Published by Thomas Nelson and Sons, London, Edinburgh, and New York.* 1857

Ballantyne enlarges on each stanza in nursery prose, and adds his own illustrations.

380 Squire Fox Went Out In a Hungry Plight. *George Waterston & Sons, Edinburgh & London.* [c. 1880]

Frogs, Waddling and Wooing

381 The Gaping, Wide-Mouthed, Waddling Frog. A New and Entertaining Game of Questions and Commands. With Proper Directions for Playing the Game, and Crying the Forfeits. Embellished with Fifteen Neatly Coloured Engravings. *London: Dean & Munday, Threadneedle-Street; and A. K. Newman & Co., Leadenhall-Street.* [1823].

382 A Gaping-wide-mouth Waddling Frog. *London: George Routledge and Sons.* [1866]

No. 61 in Routledge's New Sixpenny Toy Books. The illustrations are by Walter Crane.

383 Frog in a Cocked Hat. *Hodges, Printer (from Pitt's) Wholesale Toy Warehouse, 7 Dials.* [c. 1845]

A slip sheet.

384 Aunt Affable's Story about The Little Frog and Pretty Mouse. *London: Dean & Co, Threadneedle Street.* [c. 1845]

Tells the story of a second mouse-smitten frog, whose courtship was successful:

> I'm not like Rowley Powley, who
> Once lived, folks say, at Greenwich;
> For I'm sincere; but he, you know,
> Was gammon—all, —and spinach.

385 Aunt Busy-Bee's Little Frog and Pretty Mouse. *Dean & Son, 31 Ludgate Hill, Printers, Lithographers, and Book and Print Publishers.* [1856]

An edition of the above still with hand-coloured illustrations but in enlarged format.

386 The Frog who Would A-Wooing Go. By Charles Bennett. *London: Routledge, Warne and Routledge.* [c. 1860]

First published 1858.

387 The Frog that Would a Wooing Go. *London: Dean & Son, Juvenile Book Publishers, 11, Ludgate Hill.* [1862?]

Hand-coloured illustrations, the pictorial card cover printed in blue and gold.

388 A Frog he would a Woo-ing go. *London: Frederick Warne & Co. New York: Scribner, Welford & Armstrong.* [c. 1868]

Warne's Juvenile Drolleries, no. 7.

389 A Frog he would a-wooing go. R. Caldecott's Picture Books. *George Routledge & Sons.* Price One Shilling. [1883]

390 A Frog he would A-wooing go. Pictured by J. A. Shepherd. *London: Grant Richards, 9 Henrietta Street, Covent Garden, W.C.* [1900]

391 The Frog's Wooing. *Marcus Ward & Co. London Belfast New York.* Illustrated by E. Caldwell. [c. 1900]

The book is shaped to the contours of the Frog's head, shoulders, and quizzing glass.

392 The Frog Who Would A Wooing Go. Fairy Moonbeam's Series. *McLoughlin Bros. Publishers, New York.* [c. 1900]

A six cent picture book. The gift of Mrs Horatio Hughes.

393 The Manager turn'd an O. P. *Printed by J. Jennings, 15, Water-lane, Fleet-street, London.* [1809]

A slip song in the manner of 'A frog who would a-wooing go' celebrating the compromise reached about the Covent Garden Theatre prices, following the 'O.P.' riots. Cf no 421.

Humpty Dumpty

395 Pictorial Humpty Dumpty. Aliquis, fecit. *Tilt & Bogue, 86 Fleet Street, London.* 1843

An engraved panorama, over 5 feet long, with four translations of Humpty Dumpty on the inside front cover. Both a plain copy and a coloured copy are on view.

396 Humpty Dumpty Painting Book. Father Tuck's "Little Artists" Series. [c. 1910]

Published by Raphael Tuck & Sons Ltd. Printed in Germany.

397 Humpty Dumpty on Ice. Directed and Produced by Gerald Palmer, Empire Pool, Wembley. *Tom Arnold Presentations Ltd.* [1970]

Children's souvenir colouring book.

Jack The House Builder

398 The House that Jack Built, with Appropriate Introductions, the Music Entirely New, By an Eminent Composer. *London, Printed & Sold by C. Mitchell, 51 Southampton Row, Russell Sqre.* [1809?]

399 The History of the House that Jack Built. A Diverting Story. *London: Printed for Harris and Son, Corner of St. Paul's Church-Yard.* [1820]

Publisher's specimen pages of the fourth title in Harris's Cabinet of Amusement & Instruction.

400 The House that Jack Built; To which is added, Some Account of Jack Jingle, Showing by what Means he acquired his Learning and in consequence thereof got rich, and built himself [a] House. Adorned with Cuts. *York: Printed by J. Kendrew, Colliergate.* [c. 1820]

401 The House that Jack Built. [c. 1830]

Single sheet, to make eight pages of a picture book; before binding and cutting, but after the hand-colouring of the illustrations.

402 The House that Jack Built. *Devonport: Printed by and for Samuel and John Keys.* [c. 1835]

Advertised for sale at one half-penny.

403 The House that Jack Built; An entertaining Story, for Children. *Banbury: Printed and Sold by J. G. Rusher, Bridge-Street.* Price One Penny. [c. 1840]

404 The House that Jack Built: to which is added The Disappointment, &c. *London: Richardson and Son, 172, Fleet St.; 9, Capel Street, Dublin; and Derby. Price One Penny.* [c. 1840]

405 The House that Jack Built. *Leeds: Webb, Millington & Co.* 1849. Threepence.
Hand-coloured woodcuts.

406 This is the House that Jack Built. *London: Dean and Son, Threadneedle Street.* [c. 1850]
One of Dean's Merriment Series, and Sister Lady-Bird's Series, with hand-coloured engravings.

407 The House that Jack Built. *Printed for the Booksellers.* [*Otley: Yorkshire J. S. Publishing & Stationery Co., Limited.* c. 1850]

408 The House that Jack Built splendidly illustrated and magnificently illuminated by the Son of a Genius. [1854]
Hand-coloured illustrations by Henry George Hine, executed in the style of a child.

409 The House that Jack Built. *W. Walker & Sons, Otley.* [c. 1860]
A single sheet, 5 × 15 ins, folded to make eight pages.

410 The House that Jack built. *London: Published by Bysh & Rose, 58 & 60, Albany Road, Old Kent Road.* [c. 1862]

411 The House that Jack Built. Aunt Friendly's Coloured Picture Books. 3d. or on linen 6d. *London: F. Warne & Co.* [c. 1866]

412 The House that Jack built. One of R. Caldecott's Picture Books. *George Routledge & Sons.* One Shilling. [1878]

413 The History of the House that Jack Built, a Diverting Story. Illustrated by E. Morant Cox. *London: Griffith, Farran, Okeden & Welsh (successors to Newbery and Harris) West Corner St. Paul's Churchyard: and Sydney, N.S.W.* [c. 1890]

414 The House that Jack Built & Other Nursery Rhymes. Illustrated by Violet M. & Evelyn Holden. *Published by J. M. Dent & Co. at Aldine House in Great Eastern Street: London.* 1895
Banbury Cross Series, edited by Grace Rhys.

415 'This is Jack'. Sheet of shaped, colour-printed, relief scraps, with a line or more of the rhyme beneath each picture. [c. 1900]

416 The House that Jack Built. Drawn by 'The Pilgrims'. *London: Anthony Treherne & Co. Ltd., York Buildings, Adelphi. New York: The H. B. Claflin Company.* [c. 1905]
No. 7 in 'The Stump Books for Children. A Great Novelty in Children's Books. Size 6 in. by 1½ in. Price 1s. 6d. per vol.' These books were so narrow and thick they had tapes to fasten them when shut.

417 The House that Jack Built. [c. 1937]
A threepenny shaped book, with a front door, on the cover, which opens to reveal Jack inside a comfortable cretonne-hung 1930s house, with a uniformed maid bringing tea.

418 This is the House that Jack Built. [An Uncle Dan Book. *D. Harper & Co., Ltd., London.* c. 1947. Price 4½d.]

419 The House that Jack Built. Arranged and Illustrated by Molly B. Thomson. [1948]
A 'Kiddie Kut' Book, published by Collins The pages are shaped and cut so that the pictures are augmented by parts of the illustrations on other pages.

420 The House that Jack Built. [*Oxford University Press.* c. 1950. Price 6d.]

421 The House that Jack Built. I Spy I delt. *Pubd, Septr, 1809 by Walker No 7 Cornhill.*
Hand-coloured engraving issued at the time of the 'O.P.' riots at Covent Garden Theatre, when John Kemble 'the Manager full of scorn . . . raised the price to the people forlorn'. Cf. no. 393.

422 The Coach that Nap ran from: An Epic Poem in Twelve Books. Illustrated with Twelve Coloured Engravings. Price One Shilling and Sixpence, or, Embellished with a Ticket of Admission to the Exhibition of Buonaparte's Military Carriage, at the London Museum. Price Two Shillings. *London: Printed by Whittingham and Rowland, Goswell Street, For the Proprietor, At the Juvenile Library, London Museum, Piccadilly.* 1816.
By William Bullock, the proprietor of the Museum, which was in the newly-erected Egyptian Hall in Piccadilly. This copy is uncoloured, and has the price altered by hand to 1/6. It still contains the signed ticket of admission to the exhibition.

423 The Barn that Tom Built. A New Game of Forfeits. Embellished with Sixteen Coloured Engravings. *London: Printed and Sold by John Marshall, 140, Fleet Street, From Aldermary Church-Yard.* 1817. Price 1s. 6d.

424 The Political House that Jack Built. With Thirteen Cuts. Fiftieth Edition. *London: Printed by and for William Hone, Ludgate Hill.* 1820.

Written by Hone, illustrated by George Cruikshank, and first published in 1819, this pamphlet in favour of reform is said to have sold upwards of 100,000 copies.

425 The Palace of John Bull, Contrasted with the poor "House that Jack Built". Second Edition, with Improvements. With eight Copper-plates . . . *London, Published by Simpkins & Marshal, Stationers'-Court . . . 1820.*

426 The Crystal Palace that Fox Built. A Pyramid of Rhyme, With Nine Illustrations by John Gilbert. *London: David Bogue, 86 Fleet Street.* 1851.

Commemorates the opening of the Great Exhibition.

427 The New House that Jack Built. By Ralph Somerville. With thirty coloured illustrations by Percy J. Billinghurst. *London: Hodder & Stoughton, 27, Paternoster Row, E.C.* [1903]

The Little Ones' Library.

Jack and Jill

428 Jack and Jill, and Old Dame Gill. *York: Printed and Sold by J. Kendrew, Colliergate.* [c. 1820]

429 Jack & Jill, and Old Dame Gill. *Banbury: Printed by J. G. Rusher.* [c. 1840]

430 Jack and Jill. *W. Walker & Sons, Otley.* [c. 1860]
A single sheet, 5 × 15 ins., folded to make eight pages.

431 The Story of Jack & Jill. *Otley: William Walker and Sons.* [c. 1860].
'Coloured' edition.

Jack Horner

432 The Pleasant History of Jack Horner: Containing his Witty Tricks and Pleasant Pranks, which he play'd from his riper Years. Right Pleasant and Delightful for Winter and Summer's Recreation. *Glasgow:* Printed in the Year, M,DCCLXIV [1764].

433 The Pleasant History of Jack Horner. Containing The witty Tricks and pleasant Pranks he play'd from his Youth to his riper Years; pleasant and delightful both for Winter and Summer Recreation. *London, Printed: And sold by J. Drewry, Bookseller in Derby.* [c. 1790]

434 The Renowned History of Little Jack Horner. Illustrated with Elegant Copper-Plate Engravings. *London: Printed for the Booksellers.* Price 1s. Plain, or 1s. 6d. Coloured. [1813]

A coloured copy. The publisher was William Darton, Junr., Holborn Hill.

435 Grandmamma Easy's New Story about Little Jack Horner; and An Account of the Many Nice Things of which his Mince Pie was Made. *Dean & Co. Threadneedle Street.* [c. 1845]

An early attempt to use a nursery rhyme for educational purposes.

436 Park's History of Little Jack Horner. *London: Pub. by A. Park, 47, Leonard Street,* [Finsbury. c. 1850]

A new history in which Jack gives the remains of his pie to a beggar woman. Hand-coloured illustrations.

437 The History of Little Jack Horner. *London: T. Goode, 30, Aylesbury Street, Clerkenwell.* [c. 1860]

438 Little Jack Horner. *Goode Bros Lithrs Clerkenwell Green, E.C.* [c. 1885]

Lightheart Series no. 54. The text is similar to Park's edition, but in the illustrations Jack is shown wearing a Little Lord Fauntleroy costume.

Jack Jingle

439 Jack Jingle and Sucky Shingle. *York: Printed and Sold by J. Kendrew, Colliergate.* [c. 1825]

440 The History of Jacky Jingle. [*Devonport: Printed by and for S. & J.Keys.* c. 1835]
Advertised for sale at one half-penny.

441 The Laughable History of Little Jack Jingle. (A New Version.) *n.p.* [c. 1870]

Jack Sprat

442 The Life of Jack Sprat, His Wife, and His Cat. *York: Printed by J. Kendrew, Colliergate.* [c. 1820]

443 The Life of Jack Sprat. *Banbury: Printed by J. G. Rusher.* [c. 1840]

444 Jack Sprat. And his Cat. *Bishop & Co., Printers, 101, Houndsditch, London.* [c. 1840]

445 The Life of Little Jack Sprat. *Bishop & Co., Printers, 101, Houndsditch, London.* [c. 1840]
Same format as previous item, but different contents.

446 Jack Sprat. *London: Dean & Son, Juvenile Book Publishers, 11, Ludgate Hill.* [c. 1860]
One of Dean's New Musical Series, with hand-coloured illustrations.

447 Jack Sprat. [*London: Dean & Son. c. 1860*]
Illustrated sheet music. The engravings signed F. Staples.

Jacky Dandy

448 Jacky Dandy's Delight. *London: Printed and Sold by J. Pitts, 6, Great St. Andrew Street, 7 Dial[s].* [c. 1815]
A small 16pp chapbook.

449 Jacky Dandy's Delight: or, the History of Birds and Beasts; in Prose and Verse. Embellished with Wood-cuts. *J. Kendrew, Printer, York.* [c. 1820]

450 Jacky Dandy's Delight. *J. Roberts, Wood-Street, Leeds.* [c. 1825]

451 Jacky Dandy. *Bishop & Co., Printers, 101, Houndsditch, London.* [c. 1840]
8 pp. chapbook, the first page hand-coloured.

Jumping Joan

452 Jumping Joan. *London: Printed for S. Carvalho, 18, West Place, Nelson-street, City Road.* [c. 1825]
A small 16 pp. chapbook.

453 Jumping Joan. *London: Printed and Sold by J. E. Evans, Long Lane, Smithfield.* [c. 1830]

454 The Diverting History of Jumping Joan, and her Dog and Cat. Adorned with fine Wood Cuts. *Otley: Printed by W. Walker, at the Wharfdale Stanhope Press.* Price one Penny. [c. 1830]

Kings and Queens

455 Sing a Song of Six-pence. *London: Frederick Warne & Co.* [1866]
The ninth (as yet unnumbered) of Aunt Louisa's London Toy Books.

456 The Song of Sixpence Toy Book with Twenty-four Pages of Illustrations by Walter Crane. *London: George Routledge and Sons, Broadway, Ludgate Hill. New York: 9 Lafayette Place.* [1876]

457 Sing a Song for Sixpence. One of R. Caldecott's Picture Books. *George Routledge and Sons.* Price One Shilling. [1880]

458 King Cole. *London & Otley: William Walker & Sons.* [c. 1890]

459 The King of the Cannibal Islands. *J. Pannell, Printer, 24, Byrom-street, Liverpool.* [c. 1845]
A broadsheet.

THE

KING AND QUEEN

OF

HEARTS:

WITH THE ROGUERIES OF THE

KNAVE

WHO STOLE AWAY THE QUEEN'S PIES.

Illustrated in

FIFTEEN ELEGANT ENGRAVINGS.

LONDON:

Printed for THOMAS HODGKINGS, at the Juvenile Library, Hanway-Street, (opposite Soho-Square) Oxford-Street; and to be had of all Booksellers.

460 The King & Queen of Hearts: with the Rogueries of the Knave who Stole Away the Queen's Pies. Illustrated in Fifteen Elegant Engravings. *London: Printed for Thomas Hodgkings* [sic] *at the Juvenile Library, Hanway-Street, (opposite Soho-Square) Oxford-Street; and to be had of all Booksellers.* [1805]
The first book Charles Lamb wrote for children, of which few copies have survived; and there is reason for thinking this copy, with the misspelt name, Hodgkings for Hodgkins, is the first issue. The plates are believed to be by William Mulready.

461 Grandmamma Easy's New Story of the Queen of Hearts. *Dean & Co. Threadneedle Street.* [c. 1845]

462 The Queen of Hearts Alphabet, Illustrated by [Percy] Cruikshank. *London Published by Read, Brooks & Co., 128, Aldersgate Street, (Late 10, Johnson's Court, Fleet Street.)* [c. 1865]

One of Read's Grandmama Goodsoul's New Series of Picture Books, the 'Indestructible' edition, priced 1s. Percy Cruikshank was George Cruikshank's nephew.

463 The King, Queen, & Knave of Hearts. *London, Frederick Warne & Co.* [c. 1870]

Aunt Louisa's London Toy Books, no. 30.

464 The Queen of Hearts. One of R. Caldecott's Picture Books. *George Routledge & Sons.* [1881]

465 The Queen of Hearts. *Raphael Tuck & Sons. London, Paris, New York.* [c. 1900]

A concertina-folding series of six shaped embossed coloured scraps. The gift of Lady Bonham-Carter.

466 Queen of Hearts painting and tracing book. [*The Children's Press London and Glasgow.* 1963]

The gift of Miss Carrol Jenkins.

467 Famous Jingles. Comprising Jingles and Jokes. Queen of Hearts. Bright Thoughts. Old Dame Trot. Rich Mrs. Duck. Joyful Tales. With forty-eight illustrations, printed in colors. *New York, McLoughlin Bros.* [c. 1880]

Little Kittens

468 The Marriage of the Three Little Kittens. *London: Dean & Son, Juvenile Book Publishers, 11, Ludgate Hill.* [1860]

One of 'Dean's Children's Coloured Untearable Cloth Toy Books' sold at 1s. The text tells of the kittens' amorous adventures when they put on their mittens.

469 The Marriage of the Three Little Kittens . . . [1862]

Another edition. As well as being untearable, this edition is waterproof and washable. Sold at 1s. 6d.

470 Three Little Kittens with Coloured Pictures. Nelson's Oil Colour Picture Books for the Nursery. *T. Nelson & Sons, London & Edinburgh.* [c. 1864]

471 The 3 Little Kittens. *T. Nelson & Sons, London & Edinburgh.* [c. 1870]

472 The Three Kittens. *Ernest Nister, London. E. P. Dutton & Co., New York.* Copyright 1895.

The top of the book is shaped to the three kittens on the front cover.

473 The Three Little Kittens. *London: Dean & Son, Ld, 160A Fleet Street, E.C.* [c. 1895]

A shaped book, which opens out to become a six-panel 'screen', with pictures on one side and verses on the other.

474 The Three Little Kittens. A Tiny Tuck Book. [c. 1947. Price 2d.]

A midget book, $3\frac{3}{4} \times 2\frac{1}{2}$ ins. Printed in Canada.

475 Three Little Kittens and Other Rhymes for Little Folk. [Made in England. c. 1950. Price 4d.]

Men and Maids

476 Where are you going, my pretty maid? *Published by C. Neesom, 93, Brick Lane, Bethnal Green, near the Railway Arch. Where a Collection of Old and New Songs may be had.* [c. 1845]

A broadsheet.

477 The Milkmaid. R. Caldecott's Picture Books. *George Routledge & Sons.* One Shilling. 1882

Presentation copy from the artist, 7 Oct. 1882. Caldecott's six original paintings for this book, executed on proofs of the sepia key-blocks, are also on view.

478 Where are you going to, my pretty Maid? *Raphael Tuck & Sons, London, Paris, New York.* [c. 1900]

A concertina-folding series of six shaped embossed coloured scraps. The gift of Lady Bonham-Carter.

479 I Shall Be Married on Monday Morning. *Williamson, Printer, Newcastle.* [c. 1850]

A broadsheet. The fifth verse has entered the nursery repertoire (*ODNR* no. 464).

480 A Song. There was a little Man, and he woo'd a little Maid. Nineteenth century 'forgery' of the song sheet printed at Horace Walpole's Strawberry Hill Press in 1764.

481 Authentic Memoirs of the Little Man and the Little Maid: with some Interesting Particulars of Their Lives. Illustrated with Engravings. A New Edition. *London: Printed for John Souter, School*

Library, 73, St. Paul's Church Yard. By J. and C. Adlard, 23, Bartholomew-Close. [c. 1825]

First published by B. Tabart, 1807. 12 hand-coloured engravings.

482 The Courtship and Wedding of the Little Man and the Little Maid. Illustrated with Seven Pictures by John Absolon. *London: Sampson Low, Son, & Co., 47, Ludgate Hill.* [c. 1860]

A reprint of one of Cundall's Pleasure Books for Young Children. See no. 240.

483 The Dressed Figure Book of the Little Man & Maid. *London: Dean & Son, 65, Ludgate Hill, E.C.* [1866]

Hand-coloured illustrations with bows and skirts of real cloth added to the costumes. A rewriting of the traditional verses.

484 The Whole Particulars of that Renowned Sportsman Sam and his Gun; of his Wonderful Skill in Shooting; with a Description of his Wife Joan, surnamed Economical. *London: For Didier & Tebbett, at the Juvenile Library of English, French, and Italian Books, and Repository of Instructive Games, No. 75, St. James's Street, Pall-Mall.* 1808.

An embellished re-telling of the story of the little man who had a little gun. *ODNR* no. 325.

485 The History of Sam, The Sportsman, and his Gun, also, of His Wife Joan. Embellished with Wood-cuts. *York: Printed and Sold by J. Kendrew, Colliergate.* c. 1820

486 The History of Sam the Sportsman (From an Old Chap Book). Pictured by Frank Adams. *Blackie and Son Limited: London, Glasgow, Bombay.* [1910].

487 The Legend of the Little Man and Little Gun a Poem in seven stanzas Embellished with fourteen appropriate Designs inscribed and dedicated with permission to G. W. V * * * * * * * Esqr. "——delightful task To teach the young idea how to shoot" F. Morley invt & fecit. 1813

Privately printed booklet. The skit was written by Frances, wife of the first Earl of Morley, for her husband's 13-year-old nephew George William Frederick Villiers on the occasion, it would seem, of his being taken out shooting partridges on the 1st of September. Villiers became fourth Earl of Clarendon, and was British foreign secretary during the Crimean War.

Blind Mice

488 Three Blind Mice. With Mewsic and Words from an Early Edition. Illustrated by C. A. Doyle. Waterston's Nursery Library. *George Waterston & Sons, Edinburgh & London.* [1883]

489 Three Blind Mice. *Raphael Tuck and Sons, London, Paris, New York.* [c. 1900]

A concertina-folding series of six shaped embossed coloured scraps.

Miller of Dee

490 The King and the Miller of the Dee. *London: H. Such, Machine Printer & Publisher, 177 Union Street, Boro'.—S.E.* [c. 1850]

A broadside.

Mother Goose

491 Old Mother Goose. *London: Sold by J. Pitts, Great St. Andrew-street.* [c. 1815]

Described as a 'brave new book' this is, in fact, a small 16pp chapbook with woodcuts crudely hand-coloured.

492 Old Mother Goose; or, The Golden Egg. *London: Printed and sold by J. E. Evans, Long Lane, Smithfield.* [c. 1830]

493 The Amusing History of Mother Goose. [*Devonport: Printed by S. & J. Keys.* c. 1835]

Advertised for sale at one half-penny.

494 Mother Goose, and the Golden Egg. *Bideford: Printed for the Booksellers.* [c. 1835]

495 Park's History of Old Mother Goose, and the Golden Egg. *London: Printed by A. Park, 47, Leonard Street, Finsbury.* [c. 1840].

496 Old Mother Goose. *London: T. Goode, 30 Aylesbury-Street, Clerkenwell. Also, S. Goode, Melbourne, Port Phillip.* [c. 1855]

497 Park's Mother Goose. *A. Park, Leonard St. London.* [c. 1860]

Same cuts as no. 495, but hand-coloured and two to a page to give a large format, $9\frac{1}{2} \times 6$ ins.

498 Mother Goose. *W. Walker & Sons, Otley.* [c. 1860]

A single sheet, 5×15 ins., folded to make eight pages.

499 Mother Goose. Walkers' Toy-Books. *Otley: William Walker and Sons.* [c. 1860]

500 Mother Goose and the Golden Egg. *W. S. Fortey, (late A. Ryle,) Printer, Monmouth Court, Bloomsbury, London.* [c. 1860]

Four of the 8 woodcuts are hand-coloured.

501 Mother Goose and Her Son Jack. *Otley: William Walker and Sons.* [c. 1865]

'Coloured' edition. Two copies: one with a yellow cover, the other with a magenta cover.

502 Old Mother Goose. *London: Frederick Warne & Co.* [c. 1875]

Warne's Excelsior Toy Books, no. 69.

503 Mother Goose. Dean & Son's: Children's Pantomime Toy Books. *London: Dean & Son, 160a Fleet Street E.C.* [1881]

The performance takes place on the fourteen middle pages, which are of varying sizes so that the turning of a page partly transforms the scene. These middle pages fit within the larger picture of the stage of a theatre.

504 Mr. Simmons as Mother Goose, In the Popular new Pantomime. [1807]

Coloured engraved portrait of Samuel Simmons in the pantomime *Harlequin and Mother Goose; or, The Golden Egg*, performed at Covent Garden, 26 December 1806.

505 Mother-Goose, of Oxford. R.F. ad vivam del. *London, Publish'd May 12th 1807, by H. Humphrey, 27 St. James's Street.*

'Mother Goose', a flower-seller in Oxford, acquired her name from her likeness to Mother Goose as portrayed by Simmons (see above). The sobriquet then gave rise to the belief that the best nursery rhymes emanated from Oxford, a legend predating reality by a century and a half.

506 Mother Louse, of Louse Hall, near Oxford. Engraved from the Original Printed by David Loggan. Price 7.6. *Pubd. by C. Johnson.*

Mother Louse was a celebrated ale-house keeper in the seventeenth century. Due to accidental mis-copying or wilful misreading John Payne Collier changed her name to Goose; and subsequent writers have concluded that Mother Goose was known in England before the publication of Perrault's *Contes de la Mère Oye*. See *ODNR* pp. 39–40.

Mother Hubbard

507 Old Mother Hubbard & her Dog. [1804]

Facsimile, issued by the Oxford University Press, of Sarah Catherine Martin's illustrated manuscript. Her fourteen-verse amplification of the nursery story has been the prototype of all subsequent editions and made Mother Hubbard one of the best known characters in English literature. Had Miss Martin, who was pretty as well as witty, been a person of less responsibility, she might herself have become the subject of popular legend, for while still in her teens Prince William Henry, who was to become William IV, met her, lost his heart to her, and proposed marriage. See *ODNR*, no. 365 and plate XIII; *Oxford Book of Children's Verse*, no. 117.

508 The Comic Adventures of Old Mother Hubbard, and Her Dog: Illustrated with Fifteen Elegant Engravings on Copper-plate. *London: Printed for J. Harris, Successor to E. Newbery, at the Original Juvenile Library, the Corner of St. Paul's Church-yard.* 1805

First edition, in its original pink wrappers, of the most successful of all nursery publications: the volume that may be said to have inaugurated the profitable publishing of nonsense verse in Britain. The copy shown appears to be an early issue, with good impressions of the engravings; with the chair not replaced by the picture in the 'Hosier's' plate; but with the initials on the coffin incorrectly altered to S.M.C.

509 The Comic Adventures of Old Mother Hubbard and Her Dog . . . *London: Printed for J. Harris . . .* 1807

The twenty-fourth edition: convincing evidence of the extraordinary popularity enjoyed by this shilling booklet. The plates which have been re-engraved, not to their advantage, are of the second edition, 1806.

510 A Continuation of The Comic Adventures, of Old Mother Hubbard, and Her Dog. By S. C. M. *London, Pub. Jan. 1–1807, by J. Harris Corner of St. Paul's Church Yard.*

Twelfth edition, 1807. First published 1806. Despite its immediate success the 'Continuation' did not obtain, nor deserve, the lasting popularity of the first volume.

511 A Sequel to The Comic Adventures of Old Mother Hubbard, and Her Dog, By another Hand. *London. Published Febr. 1st 1807, by J. Harris,*

Juvenile Library, corner of St. Paul's Church Yard, and C. Knight, Windsor.

First edition, with the date 1807 on the cover. The identity of the author, whose initials W. F. appear after the dedication, is unknown.

512 The New Song Book, for Good Children. By Mother Hubbard. *Printed and Sold by G. Wood, 89 Pitt-street, Liverpool.* [c. 1810]

A midget miscellany, 16 pp., 3½ × 2½ ins, exploiting Mother Hubbard's new found popularity by naming her the editor.

513 The Comic Adventures of Old Mother Hubbard, and Her Dog: in which are shown The Wonderful Powers That Good Old Lady Possessed in the Education of Her Favourite Animal. *London: John Harris, St. Paul's Church-yard.* [c. 1827]

No.1 in Harris's Cabinet of Amusement and Instruction, first issued 1819.

514 The Comic Adventures of Old Mother Hubbard and Her Dog. Part I. Adorned with Cuts. *York: Printed by James Kendrew, Colliergate.* [c. 1820]

515 Old Mother Hubbard, and Her Dog. Embellished with Fifteen neatly-coloured Engravings. *London: Dean and Munday, Threadneedle-Street; and A. K. Newman & Co., Leadenhall-Street. Price Sixpence.* [c. 1835]

516 Old Mother Hubbard and Her Dog. *Banbury: Printed by J. G. Rusher.* [c. 1840]

Illustrations in this chapbook are reproduced in *ONRB* pp. 28–30.

517 Old Mother Hubbard and her Dog. *Printed and Published by G. Ingram, 41, Old Street, St. Luke, E.C.* [c. 1840]

518 Mother Hubbard and her Dog. *London: Printed for the Booksellers.* [c. 1840]

519 Mother Hubbard and Her Dog: To which is added The History of Tom Tucker. *London: Richardson and Son, 172, Fleet St.; 9, Capel Street, Dublin; and Derby. Price One Penny.* [c. 1840]

520 Old Mother Hubbard, and Her Dog. Embellished with Beautiful Coloured Plates. *Glasgow: Published by J. Lumsden & Son.* [c. 1845]

One of Lumsden's Improved Twopenny Books. The illustrations are hand-coloured.

521 Mother Hubbard. *London: J. Rosewarne, 83, Houndsditch and Bridge-street, Belper.* [c. 1850]

522 Mother Hubbard. *Printed for the Booksellers.* [*Otley: Yorkshire J. S. Publishing & Stationery Co., Limited.*] [c. 1850]

523 The Adventures of Mother Hubbard and her Clever Dog. [*W. Walker & Sons*] *London and Otley.* [c. 1855]

One of 'Walkers' New Series of Untearable Toy-Books'. The pages mounted on linen, with hand-coloured illustrations. The rhyme has been rewritten so that eight lines describe each illustration instead of two.

524 The Moveable Mother Hubbard. *London: Dean & Son. Printers & Publishers, 11, Ludgate Hill.* [1857]

Animation is achieved by a tab protruding beneath each picture. In the left-hand picture on view not only do both Mother Hubbard and her dog move when the tab is pulled, but the dog's reflection moves in the mirror. The illustrations are hand-coloured.

525 Old Mother Hubbard and her Wonderful Dog. *London: Printed and Published at W. S. Fortey's Whole-sale Juvenile Book Warehouse, 2 & 3, Monmouth Court, Bloomsbury, W.C.* [1859]

526 Old Mother Hubbard, and her Dog. *London: Dean & Son, 11, Ludgate Hill.* [1860]

The red and gold illustration printed on the paper cover may be compared with the hand-coloured illustration in *Mother Hubbard, and Other Old Friends* (no. 101). The full-page illustrations within are hand-coloured.

527 A New Story about Mother Hubbard and Her Dog. *London: Ward & Lock, 158, Fleet Street.* [1860?]

'Moveable Edition, Price Two Shillings.' Animation is achieved in the same way as in Dean's Moveable Mother Hubbard.

528 Old Mother Hubbard. *George Routledge and Sons, London and New York.* [c. 1860]

One of 'Routledge's Threepenny Toy-Books with Six Coloured Illustrations, Printed by Kronheim'.

529 Old Mother Hubbard. *London: Darton & Co. Holborn Hill.* [c. 1860]

The engravings, which are crudely colour-printed, are by Calvert.

530 Mother Hubbard. *W. Walker & Sons, Otley.* [c. 1860]

A single sheet, 5 × 15 ins., folded to make eight pages.

531 Mother Hubbard and Her Dog. *Otley: William Walker & Sons.* [c. 1860]

A rewritten version. Alternate openings in colour.

532 Old Mother Hubbard and her Dog. *T. Nelson & Sons, London & Edinburgh.* [c. 1865]

Almost certainly illustrated by Alfred Crowquill (A. H. Forrester).

533 Mother Hubbard's Grand Party. *London. Dean & Son, Ludgate Hill, E.C.* [1866]

Written and illustrated by J. V. Barrett. The first of Dean's Young England's Large 4to Oil-Colour and Gold Picture Toy Books. The liberal use of gold in the illustrations is partial compensation for the advertisement beneath the 11 × 19 ins. centrespread illustration.

534 Panorama of Mother Hubbard. *W. Walker & Sons, Otley.* [c. 1870]

A rewritten version. Opens out to 5½ feet.

535 Old Mother Hubbard and her Dog. *London: Frederick Warne & Co.* [c. 1872]

Warne's Excelsior London Toy Books: New Series, no. 4.

536 Old Mother Hubbard. One of the four titles in The Marquis of Carabas' Picture Book . . . Illustrations by Walter Crane. *London: George Routledge and Sons, The Broadway, Ludgate. New York: 416 Broome Street.* [1874]

537 Old Mother Hubbard. Magical Changes with Mother Goose' Melodies. *G. W. Carleton & Co. Publishers. New York.* Copyright 1879 by Donaldson Brothers.

Magic Mother Goose Series no. 4. The story of Mother Hubbard is depicted by William Ludwell Sheppard in a series of sepia drawings, with flaps which, when turned over, show what the dog was doing when Mother Hubbard returned. In one it appears Mother Hubbard's visit to the alehouse was not solely for the dog's benefit.

538 Mother Hubbard. By Marrion. *London: Augener & Co. 86, Newgate Street.* [c. 1880]

Sheet music. The coloured litho on the cover is by R. J. Hamerton.

539 Old Mother Hubbard and Her Comical Dog. *London, Ward, Lock & Co.* [c. 1880].

540 Mother Hubbard. *W. Walker & Sons (Otley) Ltd.* [c. 1900]

A cheaply produced 8 pp. booklet, with a rather lame re-rhyming of the story.

541 'Old Mother Hubbard.' Sheet of sixteen colour-printed, shaped, relief scraps, with a verse beneath each picture. [c. 1900]

542 Old Mother Hubbard. Dean's Holiday Series No. 85 Mounted on Cotton Cloth. *London: Dean & Son, Ltd., Debrett House, 29, King Street, W.C.2.* [c. 1915]

Illustrated by Gordon Robinson.

543 Aunt Affable's Story of Old Mother Bantry and Her Cat. *London: Dean & Co. Threadneedle St.* [c. 1845]

Mother Bantry is a near relation of Mother Hubbard, and went to the pantry to get her cat, Grip, some meat.

544 Dame Bantry and her Cat. *London: Dean & Son, 11 Ludgate Hill.* [1858]

Dame Bantry has here been put into larger format in Grandpapa Easy and Grandmama Easy's Series.

545 The Comical Story of Old Dame Bantry and her Cat. *London & Otley. William Walker & Sons.* [c. 1865]

Illustrations printed in four colours.

Peter Piper

546 Peter Piper's Practical Principles of Plain and Perfect Pronunciation. To which is added, a Collection of Moral and Entertaining Conundrums. *London: John Harris, Corner of St. Paul's Churchyard.* [c. 1824]

No. 7 in Harris's Cabinet of Amusement and Instruction, first issued 1820.

547 Peter Piper's Practical Principles of Plain and Perfect Pronunciation. *London: Grant Richards.* 1902.

Dumpy Books for Children, no. 17.

548 Peter Piper's: Practical Principles of Plain & Perfect Pronunciation. Pictured by Wyndham Payne. *London. Published by John Lane, The Bodley Head Ltd., in Vigo Street,* 1926.

Little Pigs

549 This Little Pig went to Market. *London: George Routledge & Sons.* [1869]

No. 97 in Routledge's New Sixpenny Toy Books. Illustrated by Walter Crane.

550 This Little Pig went to Market. *George Routledge & Sons.* [c. 1874]

Routledge's Shilling Toy Books, no. 7, first published c. 1865.

551 This Little Pig Went to Market. Walter Crane's Picture Books Re-issue. *London: John Lane. Chicago: Stone & Kimball.* [1895]

552 The Five Little Pigs. Cut-Outs Designed by Edwin La Dell. *London: John Miles, Amen Corner, E.C.4.* [c. 1938]

The cut-out pictures of the pigs are hinged to form a panorama.

Simple Simon

553 The History of Simple Simon. *York: Printed by J. Kendrew, Colliergate.* [c. 1820]

554 Simple Simon. *Printed and Sold by T. Batchelar, 14, Hackney Road Crescent.* [c. 1825]

555 Park's History of Simple Simon. *London: Printed by A. Park, 47, Leonard Street, Finsbury.* [c. 1840]

Four of the eight woodcuts have rudimentary colouring by the publisher.

556 The History of Simple Simon. *Printed and Published at Paul's General Printing Office, 18, Great St. Andrew Street, Broad Street, Bloomsbury, sold by C. Neesom, 166, Brick Lane, Spitalfields.* [c. 1840].

A crude imitation of Park's edition above.

557 Park's Amusing History of Simple Simon. *London: Printed by A. Park, 47, Leonard Street, Finsbury.* [c. 1850].

A refurbished edition of no. 555, with newly designed cover, and well-coloured woodcuts.

558 Park's History of Simple Simon. *London: Printed by A. Park, 47, Leonard Street, Finsbury.* [c. 1852]

A further edition, the size increased to 6⅛ × 8⅜ ins. to have two illustrations on each page. One of Park's Library of Instruction and Amusement.

559 Simple Simon. Marcus Ward's Royal Illuminated Nursery Rhymes [no. 4.]. *Published by W. P. Nimmo, Edinburgh.* [c. 1872]

560 The Story of Simple Simon. Illustrated by Frank Adams. *Blackie & Son Limited, London, Glasgow, Dublin, Bombay.* [c. 1908]

561 Simple Simon. [*Blackie & Son, Ltd., Glasgow.* 1938?]

A later edition, showing how long such a book might be kept in print.

562 History of Simple Simon. A Bantam Picture Book. *Transatlantic Arts Ltd., 45, Great Russell Street, London and New York.* [1944]

The illustrations are from Park's 'Amusing History of Simple Simon', no. 557.

Tom the Piper's Son

563 Tom, The Piper's Son. With all the fun, That he had done. And how at last he went to France, To teach great Bonaparte to dance. *Printed and Sold by J. Pitts, 6, St. Andrew-street.* [c. 1815]

A small 16pp chapbook, the woodcuts crudely hand-coloured.

564 Tom, The Piper's Son. With all the fun, That he had done. And how at last he went to France, To teach great Bonaparte to dance. *York: Printed by J. Kendrew, Colliergate.* [c. 1820]

As in other chapbook editions, the pig Tom stole and ate is shown to have been one made of paste and currants. *ODNR* no. 510 and plate XXI.

565 Tom, The Piper's Son, With all the fun That he has done. *Devonport: Printed by and for Samuel and John Keys.* [c. 1835]

Advertised for sale at one half-penny.

566 Tom the Piper's Son. *London and Otley: Wm Walker and Son.* [c. 1845]

A title in The Illuminated Library for the Homes of Happy Childhood. A rewritten history which adds the detail that the pigs, 'well stuff'd with raisins,' are home-made:

They're made by my wife,
And my daughter, and me.

567 Tom, the Piper's Son. Walker's Toy Books. *London and Otley: William Walker and Sons.* [c. 1860]

568 Tom the Piper's Son. *W. Walker & Sons, Otley.* [c. 1860]

A single sheet, 5 × 15 ins, folded to make eight pages.

569 Panorama of Tom the Piper's Son. *W. Walker & Sons, Otley.* [c. 1870]

An elongated edition both textually and physically: the story is retold in 96 lines of verse, and the panorama opens to 5½ feet.

570 Tom, Tom, was a Piper's Son. Illustrated by William Foster. *London: Frederick Warne & Co., and New York.* [c. 1890]

571 Tom, Tom, the Piper's Son. A Tiny Tuck Book. [c. 1947. Price 2d.]

A midget booklet, 3¾ × 2½ ins. Printed in Canada.

Tommy Tucker

572 The History of Little Tom Tucker. *York: J. Kendrew, Printer, Colliergate.* [c. 1820]

573 Little Tom Tucker. *London: Printed by J. Catnach, 2 & 3, Monmouth Court, 7 Dials.* [c. 1830]

574 Tom Tucker. *Bishop & Co., Printers, 101, Houndsditch, London.* [c. 1840]

8pp chapbook, the first page hand-coloured.

575 Little Tom Tucker. *London: Printed and Published at W. S. Fortey's Wholesale Juvenile Book Warehouse, 2 & 3, Monmouth Court, Bloomsbury. W.C.* [c. 1860]

A new printing of Catnach's edition (no. 573), with Fortey's announcement, dated 1859, that he has taken over the Catnach Press.

576 Little Tom Tucker. *London: Printed and Published at W. S. Fortey's Wholesale Juvenile Book Warehouse, 4 Great St Andrew Street, Seven Dials, W.C.* [c. 1885]

A further issue of Catnach's edition. The original cuts are surrounded by a decorative border to enable the publication to become a now-fashionable quarto. Fortey did not move to Great St. Andrew Street until 1882, so the illustrations had apparently already been in use for fifty years.

577 Little Tom Tucker. *London & Otley, William Walker & Sons.* [c. 1890]

Little Market Woman

578 The Little Market Woman. *Published Novr. 25, 1784, by J. Wallis, No. 16, Ludgate Street.*

Engraved pictorial broadside 14 × 10 ins. This is the earliest known publication of the tale.

579 The Little Woman and the Pedlar: With the Strange Distraction that Seized Her, and the Undutiful Behaviour of her Little Dog on That Occasion. Illustrated in Fifteen Elegant Engravings. *London: Printed for Thomas Hodgkins, at the Juvenile Library, Hanway-Street, (opposite Soho-Square) Oxford-Street; and to be had of all Book-sellers. 1806. Price 1s. Plain; or 1s. 6d. Coloured.*

No. 2 in Godwin's Copperplate Series, the first of which was Lamb's *King and Queen of Hearts* (no. 460). The plates are believed to be by Mulready. This is a 'plain' copy.

580 The Little Woman and the Pedlar: With the Strange Distraction that Seized Her . . . *London: Printed for M. J. Godwin, at the Juvenile Library, 41, Skinner Street, Snow Hill; and to be had of all Book-sellers. 1813. Price 1s. Plain, or 1s. 6d. Coloured.*

A new edition, with the illustrations either retouched or newly engraved. William Godwin is no longer trading under the name of his manager, Hodgkins, but of his wife, Mary Jane.

581 The Little Woman and The Pedlar. *Joseph Roberts, Wood Street, Leeds.* (c. 1825)

Three of the woodcuts in this chapbook are reproduced in *ONRB* p. 169.

582 The Old Woman and the Pedlar. Illustrated by Richard Chopping. [Bantam Picture Book No. 14. *Transatlantic Arts, Ltd., London: 45 Great Russell Street, W.C.1. And New York. 1944. Price 4d*]

Old Woman who bought a Pig

583 A True History of a Little Old Woman, who found a Silver Penny. *London: Printed for Tabart and Co. at the Juvenile and School Library, 157, New Bond-Street; and to be had of all Booksellers. C. Squire, Printer, Furnival's-Inn-Court, Holborn. 1806*

Full-page hand-coloured engravings, the last four being arranged as an unfolding panorama showing the unravelling of the old woman's difficulties.

584 A True History of a Little Old Woman, who found a Silver Penny. *London: Printed for Tabart and Co. at the Juvenile and School Library, New*

Bond-Street; and to be had of all Booksellers. W. Marchant, Printer, 3, Greville-Street, Holborn. 1808

Second edition, also with coloured engravings and panorama.

585 The Remarkable Adventures of An Old Woman and Her Pig. An Ancient Tale in a Modern Dress. *London: John Harris, Corner of St. Paul's Church-Yard.* [c. 1827]

Harris's Cabinet of Amusement and Instruction.

586 The Little Old Woman and her Silver Penny. *London: Dean & Son, 11, Ludgate Hill, Printers, Lithographers, and Book and Print Publishers.* [1858]

587 The Old Woman and Silver Penny. *Published by J. March, 12, Webber St. Blackfriars Road.* [c. 1860]

March's Penny Library, no. 22. 2 illustrations colour-printed.

588 The Old Woman and her Pig with drawings by John Harwood. A Baby Puffin Book. [1945]

Old Woman who Lived in a Shoe

589 The Old Woman who Lived in her Shoe. *Published by Cowan & Standring, 8 & 9 Finsbury Street, Finsbury Sqr, London.* [c. 1855]

A title in The Album Series of Children's Picture Books. The full-page hand-coloured illustrations are after designs by J. R. Barfoot.

590 The Old Woman that lived in a Shoe. From Coloured Designs by W. J. Webb. *London: Frederick Warne & Co.* [c. 1880]

Aunt Louisa's London Toy Books, no. 102. Mounted on linen.

591 Two Well-Worn Shoe Stories. Pictured by John Hassall and Cecil Aldin. *London: Sands & Co.* 1899

The first part, with separate title-page, consists of 'There was an Old Woman who lived in a Shoe,' pictured by John Hassall, 1899; the second part 'Cock-a-doodle-do' (*ODNR* no. 108) pictured by Cecil Aldin, 1899. 15 × 9¾ ins.

592 Two Simple Tales for Simple Folks by H. S. Stirling. With Twenty-two Coloured Pictures by John Hassall and Cecil Aldin. *London: Sands & Co.* [1904]

The two tales are the same as in the previous volume, and are illustrated by the same two artists; but the tales have been highly embroidered, while the size of the book is only 3¾ × 2¾ ins.

Old Woman Tossed in a Basket

593 The Flight of The Old Woman who was Tossed up in a Basket. Sketched & Etched by Aliquis. *Published by D. Bogue, 86 Fleet Street, London.* 1844

A hand-coloured panorama over 7 feet long when extended. *ODNR* no. 545 and plate XXIV.

Yankee Doodle

594 The Story of Yankee Doodle. *McLoughlin Bros. Publishers, New York.* [c. 1885]

A 58-verse history ending:
Now boys and girls, all gather 'round—
Come on, the whole 'caboodle,'
And give three cheers for Uncle Sam,
For he is Yankee Doodle.

Duke of York

595 The Brave Old Duke of York. With Illustrations by T. Butler-Stoney. *London: Sands & Co.* 1901

6 Two Alphabets

Rhyming alphabets are not as popular today as they were in the eighteenth and nineteenth centuries, when they were thought a convenient way to cover a subject comprehensively—literally from A to Z. These alphabets were of various types, didactic, informative, satiric, or purely nonsensical; and we probably have more than fifty different ones in our collection. We give here editions only of the two that have long been the favourites of the nursery, and which most happily feature together in the first exhibit.

596 THE CHILD'S NEW PLAY-THING: Being a Spelling-Book Intended To make the Learning to Read, a Diversion instead of a Task..The Fourth Edition . . . Designed for the Use of Schools, or for Children before they go to School. *London: Printed for M. Cooper at the Globe in Pater-noster-Row.* 1745

First published 1742. A remarkable primer which leads the child into learning rather than pushes him. Issued by Mary Cooper who in 1744 published the first nursery rhyme book, it contains 'a new-invented Alphabet for children to play with', consisting of a folding sheet (here intact) printed on both sides, to be cut into squares so that one letter of the alphabet appears on each square, together with the appropriate line of 'A was an archer, and shot at a frog'. On the back of this sheet is the alphabet 'A was an apple pie.' No copy of this edition is recorded by Alston.

A was an Apple Pie

597 The Tragical Death of a Apple-Pye, who was Cut in Pieces and Eat by Twenty Five Gentlemen with whom All Little People ought To be very well acquainted. *Printed by John Evans, 42, Long-lane, West-smithfield, London.* [c. 1791]

This is one of the new style of chapbook which was to remain popular for the next fifty years. It consists of a single sheet, 7 × 9 ins, folded to make sixteen pages, 3½ × 2¼ ins, a smaller size than hitherto, but in keeping with the superior publications for children already issued for some while by Newbery, Marshall, and others.

598 The History of an Apple-Pie. Written by Z. *London: Printed for Harris and Son, Corner of St. Paul's Church-Yard.* [1820]

Publisher's specimen pages of the sixth title in Harris's Cabinet of Amusement and Instruction.

599 Mark's History of an Apple Pie. King Pippin's Alphabet for Good Children. [c. 1830]

600 The History of an Apple Pie. *London: Darton & Clark.* Price Sixpence. Coloured Plates. [c. 1840]

601 The Apple-Pie Alphabet. *Published by John and Charles Mozley, Derby; and Paternoster Row, London.* Price One Penny. [c. 1845]

The Apple-Pie Alphabet is, of course, 'A was an apple-pie'; but most of the space in this chapbook and all but one of the illustrations are devoted to 'A was an Archer'.

602 The History of an Apple Pie. With Coloured Illustrations. *London: Griffith and Farran, Late Grant and Griffith, Successors to Newbery and Harris, Corner of St. Paul's Churchyard.* [c. 1856]

'Durable' edition, mounted on linen. A reprint of Harris's Cabinet of Amusement and Instruction (no. 598).

603 Darton's Indestructible The Apple Pie. Price One Shilling. [c. 1860]

604 The History of A, Apple Pie. *London: Dean & Son, Printers, Lithographers, and Book and Print Publishers, 11, Ludgate Hill.* [1861]

One of 'Dean's Untearable Cloth Children's Colored Toy Books.—1s.' Hand-coloured illustrations. Compare with Dean's *A was an Archer*, 1867 or 68.

605 A. Apple Pie. *London: Frederick Warne & Co.* [c. 1865]

The second (as yet unnumbered) of Aunt Louisa's London Toy Books.

606 A Apple Pie. By Kate Greenaway. *London. Frederick Warne & Co. Ltd. & New York.*

A 1945 printing of the book first issued in 1886 by Routledge.

607 The History of A Apple Pie. *George Routledge & Sons* [c. 1900]

The illustrations depict more than seventy-five children in contemporary costume.

608 the tragical death of a. apple pie who was cut in pieces, and eaten by twenty-six little villains [*The Shoestring Press, Whitstable.* 1966]

A concertina-folded book, 12 feet long when extended. Designed, illustrated with lino cuts, and hand-printed by Ben Sands. Limited edition, 225 copies, signed.

A was an Archer

609 Tom Thumb's Play-Thing. Being a New & Pleasant Method to allure Little Ones into the First Principles of Learning; With Cuts well adapted to each Letter in the Alphabet. As brought into Easy Verse, for the Instruction & Entertainment of Children. Part the First. *Printed by Howard and Evans, 42 Long Lane, West-smithfield, London.* [c. 1800]

A 16 pp. chapbook, 3½ × 2¼ ins., consisting only of two rhyming alphabets, the first being 'A was an Archer'. The second is more unusual, e.g.,

'Q was a Queen
That kept many sluts'.

610 Tom Thumb's Play-Book, to Teach Children their Letters as soon as they can speak: or, Easy Lessons for Little Children and Beginners. Being A new and pleasant Method to allure Little Ones into the first Principles of Learning. *Newcastle: Printed by George Angus, in the Side.* 1824.

A provincial edition of a primer first published in 1747. Contains 'A was an Archer' with a woodcut illustration for each letter.

611 The Hobby-Horse, or the High Road to Learning: Being a Revival of That Favourite Alphabet "A was an Archer, and shot at a Frog". *London: Printed for J. Harris and Son, Corner of St. Paul's Church-Yard.* 1820

Publisher's specimen pages of the eleventh title in Harris's Cabinet of Amusement and Instruction.

612 The Hobby-Horse . . . *London: John Harris, Corner of St. Paul's Church-yard.* [c. 1827]

A later edition, with the illustrations framed and background filled in with colour.

613 The Easter Gift; being a Useful Toy for Little Miss & Master to learn their ABC. *J. Catnach, Printer, 2, & 3, Monmouth Court, 7 Dials.* [c. 1825]

614 The Picture Alphabet. *London: Richardson and Son, 172, Fleet St.; 9, Capel Street, Dublin; and Derby. Price One Penny.* [c. 1840]

Contains both 'A Apple-pie' and 'A was an Archer'. For the woodcuts, which are probably by Orlando Jewitt, see *ONRB* pp. 106–7.

615 A was an Archer. *London: Sold by the Booksellers.* [c. 1840]

616 A was an Archer. *Derby: Printed by and for Henry Mozley and Sons. Price One Halfpenny.* [c. 1840]

617 Tom Thumb's Alphabet. Illustrated by W. McConnell. Engraved by the Brothers Dalziel. [*London: David Bogue, 86, Fleet Street. c. 1855*]

618 The Shilling Alphabet: Tom Thumb's. *George Routledge & Sons, Broadway, Ludgate Hill, London.* [c. 1865]

Routledge's Shilling Toy Books, no. 8. McConnell's illustrations here appear in colour.

619 A Was An Archer. *London: Dean & Son, Publishers & Printers, 65 Ludgate Hill, E.C.* [1867 or 68]

Illustrations by J. V. Barret. One of the first of Dean's Infantile Oil-Colour Picture Toy Books. Compare Dean's *History of A, Apple Pie*, 1861.

620 Routledge's Coloured ABC Book . . . with Twenty-four Pages of Illustrations. By Kronheim and others. *London: George Routledge and Sons, The Broadway, Ludgate. New York: 416, Broome Street.* [c. 1873]

Contains four alphabets, one being McConnell's 'Tom Thumb's Alphabet'. See above.

7 Histories and Interpretations

The popular belief that nursery rhymes are either wonderfully old or have hidden meanings—or, sometimes, that they are both old and cryptic—may itself be of some antiquity. William King in 1709 was probably reflecting the commonroom speculations of his day when he made-believe 'Boys and girls come out to play' was to be found in ancient Greek and Latin texts (see no. 7). And as can be seen here the quasi-intellectual sport of giving nursery rhymes secret histories or meanings has continued into our own time. Who today has not heard the story (and been tempted to pass it on) that the rhyme 'Ring-a-ring o' roses' dates from the Great Plague?

> *Ring-a-ring o' roses,*
> *A pocket full of posies,*
> *A-tishoo! A-tishoo!*
> *We all fall down.*

A rosy rash, we are told, was a symptom of the plague, posies of herbs (sometimes of roses) were carried as protection, sneezing was the final fatal symptom, and all fall down was exactly what happened.

Our reluctance to disbelieve in whatever speculation is most marvellous is no less strong today—as any folklorist knows—than it was in days gone by, and keeps the story alive. Yet even if the rhyme accurately described the characteristics of bubonic plague in seventeenth-century terms (which it does not), no evidence exists to link it with Stuart England. The rhyme has not been found before the nineteenth century; dialect recordings suggest the wording has altered over the years; and Continental versions indicate the song had joyous rather than morbid associations (see ODNR no. 443).

It will be noticed that each of the early essays on nursery rhymes were in one way or another facetious, e.g. WilliamKing's in 1709, already referred to, B. N. Turner's in 1797 (no. 24), and the 'Critical Comments on the Bo-peepeid' in 1807 (no. 13). In fact the only commentary on nursery rhymes before 1842 which was not humorous was demented: Bellenden Ker's Archaiology [sic] of Nursery Rhymes, 1834.

621 THE MICROCOSM, A Periodical Work, by Gregory Griffin, Of the College of Eton. *Windsor: Published for C. Knight, Castle-Street; And Sold by Mess. Robinsons, Pater-noster-Row; and Mr. Debrett, Piccadilly, London.* 1787.

The two issues dated 12 February consist of a mock criticism of 'The Queen of Hearts' written by the precocious George Canning, then aged sixteen. *The Microcosm,* incidentally, was the first school magazine; and one of the outstanding school magazines of all time.

622 ANONYMOUS. 'On Nursery Rhymes in General.' Blackwood's Edinburgh Magazine, *Edinburgh: William Blackwood, no. 17, Prince's Street,* vol. XVI, July 1824, pp. 71–3.
A skit on Hazlitt.

623 JOHN BELLENDEN KER. An Essay on the Archaiology [sic] of Popular English Phrases and Nursery Rhymes. *Southampton: Fletcher and Son. London: Black, Young, & Young, Tavistock Street.* 1834
Considering nursery rhymes to be 'unmeaning metrical farragos' in their present wording, Ker reconstituted them in an early form of Dutch (known only to himself), Dutch being 'the nearest surviving representative of the Low-Saxon stage of our language'. He then translated the results into English, and found 'they all turned out to be anti-tithe Pasquinades and anti-monkisms'. Ker stands out as one of the most accomplished of all shapers of facts to fit theories, even when judged amongst the craftsmen of today.

624 JOHN BELLENDEN KER. A Supplement to the Two Volumes of the Second Edition of the Essay on the Archaeology of our Popular Phrases, Terms, and Nursery Rhymes. [Vol. I, II] *Andover: Printed by John King, High Street.* 1840
The bibliography of this work is appropriately complex. A second edition appeared in two volumes, 1835–1837, the first volume of which appears to be identical to a 'New Edition' of the same date. The two-volume *Supplement* here, which boldly includes a review from *The Spectator* stating that Ker's work was 'the clearest case of literary mania we remember', was also published by James Ridgway, 169 Piccadilly, in 1840–42; and we possess a further copy of vol. I (not that it is of any interest) with yet another title-page. Unhappily, however, some twentieth century commentators have not been as discriminating as was *The Spectator* in the days of our forefathers.

625 JAMES ORCHARD HALLIWELL. Popular Rhymes and Nursery Tales: a Sequel to the Popular Rhymes of England. *London: John Russell Smith, 4, Old Compton Street, Soho Square.* 1849
Although Halliwell had before him the good example of Robert Chambers whose manner he adopted (see no. 38), this volume can be said to be the first interpretative work on nursery rhymes that is neither facetious nor lunatic. It is a remarkable gathering of traditional rhymes and tales with a fact-packed commentary, the outcome of singular erudition. Had Halliwell only been a little more scrupulous about his sources and material (not everything here is precisely as it appears to be), and had he been a little more generous with his time, he might have produced a classic study of English folklore. The work was in print for many years (see no. 46).

626 JAMES ORCHARD HALLIWELL. A Catalogue of Chap-books, Garlands, and Popular Histories, in the possession of James Orchard Halliwell, Esq. *London: For Private Circulation.* 1849
Inscribed presentation copy, included here to show Halliwell's hand and character. In giving this copy to T. Crofton Croker, Halliwell emphasises the limited number printed, its (contrived) scarcity, and its current market value. Croker, whose *Fairy Legends and Traditions of the South of Ireland* had appeared when Halliwell was a child, was on the Council of the Percy Society, which published the original edition of *The Nursery Rhymes of England;* and was the man who lent Halliwell Henry Carey's nurserically-important tract *Namby Pamby* (no. 8).

627 [WILLIAM HEWSON]. Old Nursery Rhymes, of Mithraic Origin, Illustrated from the Typical Structure of the Greek-Egyptian Dial with Steps, Brought from Alexandria, and now in the British Museum. With passing remarks on the Philosophy of the Ancient Hindus respecting their Mundane Egg; Also, on the Typical Structure of the Theatre & Amphitheatre at Arles; etc., etc. 1869
The first of eight pamphlets by the Rev. William Hewson, M.A., Vicar of Goathland, published under the general title *The Hebrew and Greek Scriptures, Compared with Oriental History, Dialling, Science, and Mythology* (London: Simpkin and Co., and others) 1870. The pussy cat in the well 'may have reference to the proverbial maxim of the ancients "*in puteo veritas*" or truth lies concealed'; and the Mundane Egg, predictably, turns out to be Humpty Dumpty.

628 A. D. T. WHITNEY. Mother Goose for Grown Folks. A New, Revised, and Enlarged Edition. Illustrated by Augustus Hoppin and Hammatt Billings. *Loring, Publisher, 319 Washington Street, Boston.* [1870]
Philosophical thoughts, in verse, on the old

nursery rhymes. 'Ding, dong, bell,' for instance, evokes some sound observations, beginning:

> There never was a drama of sorrow
>> But good folks might be found, I'm afraid,
> Who a queer satisfaction could borrow
> From the parts of importance they played.

629 MARY SENIOR CLARK. The Lost Legends of the Nursery Songs. Illustrated from the Author's Designs. *London: George Bell and Sons, York Street, Covent Garden.* 1878

Imaginary tales written for the young. Estella Canziani's copy, with her bookplate.

630 WILLIAM H. WHITMORE. The Original Mother Goose's Melody, as First Issued by John Newbery, of London, about A.D., 1760. Reproduced in *fac-simile* from the edition as reprinted by Isaiah Thomas, of Worcester, Mass. about A.D., 1785, with Introductory Notes. *Albany: Joel Munsell's Sons.* 1889

Although dated 1889 on the title-page the Preface is dated Sept. 6th, 1890.

631 WILLIAM H. WHITMORE. The Original Mother Goose's Melody, as issued by John Newbery, of London, *circa* 1760; Isaiah Thomas, of Worcester, Mass., *circa* 1785, and Munroe & Francis, of Boston, *circa* 1825. Reproduced in fac-simile, from the first Worcester edition, with Introductory Notes. To which are added The Fairy Tales of Mother Goose . . . *Damrell & Upham, The Old Corner Bookstore, Boston. Griffith Farran & Co., Limited, Newbery House, London:* 1892

An expanded edition of the above, the Preface being an honest if somewhat muddled attempt to sort out the early history of nursery rhyme publishing, particularly in the United States.

632 PERCY B. GREEN. A History of Nursery Rhymes. *London: Greening & Co., Ltd., 20, Cecil Court, Charing Cross Road.* 1899

One of those books which instead of adding to its subject seems to diminish it.

633 WILLIAM FRANCIS PRIDEAUX. Mother Goose's Melody. A Facsimile Reproduction of the Earliest Known Edition. With an Introduction and Notes by Colonel W. F. Prideaux, C.S.I. *London: A. H. Bullen, 47 Great Russell Street.* 1904

The facsimile, which is of the 1791 edition (see no. 19), is supported by a sound introduction and by careful notes on individual rhymes.

634 LINA ECKENSTEIN. Comparative Studies in Nursery Rhymes. By Lina Eckenstein, author of "Woman under Monasticism". *London: Duckworth & Co. 3 Henrietta Street, Covent Garden.* 1906

A well-written, mind-stretching essay, soundly based on a study of foreign parallels and of the early nursery rhyme books.

635 HENRY BETT. Nursery Rhymes and Tales, Their Origin and History. *Methuen & Co. Ltd. 36 Essex Street W.C. London.* 1924

A competent summary of the facts as known at the time, unenhanced by original research.

636 DWIGHT EDWARDS MARVIN. Historic Child Rhymes. A Monograph on the Origin and Growth of the Rhymes That Children Use and Love. *Norwell, Massachusetts: The Ross Bookmakers.* 1930

A useful book for thesis writers wishing to enlarge their bibliographies.

637 KATHERINE ELWES THOMAS. The Real Personages of Mother Goose. Illustrated. *Lothrop, Lee & Shepard Co. [Boston.* 1930]

Although the nine errors in the transcription of the first quotation in this book, and the six errors in the second quotation (together with an incorrect reference), may not in themselves be felt serious, the reader may be made wary of accepting at face value the 343 pages and 305 references that follow.

638 WALT DISNEY'S The Truth About Mother Goose. *Published by Dell Publishing Co., Inc., 261 Fifth Ave., New York 16, N.Y. Copyright 1957, by Walt Disney Productions.*

A 10 cent comic-strip booklet, apparently produced under the spell of *The Real Personages of Mother Goose*, which may be felt to be one of Walt Disney's fantasies rather than documentaries. Gift of Professor Morris Silverman.

639 VINCENT STARRETT. 'Much Ado About Mother Goose' in Bookman's Holiday, The Private Satisfactions of an Incurable Collector. *Random House, New York.* 1942

A stimulating essay on the identity of Mother Goose, earlier published separately as *All About Mother Goose*, Apellicon Press, 1930.

640 V. SACKVILLE-WEST. Nursery Rhymes. *London: The Dropmore Press.* 1947

Edition limited to 550 copies. The value of this lively monograph lies in the fact that, for once, a gifted writer and poet is discoursing on nursery rhymes, their histories, and their place in childhood. Inserted in the volume are letters from the author written while the work was in progress.

641 V. SACKVILLE-WEST. Nursery Rhymes. With Drawings by Philippe Jullian. *London: Michael Joseph.* [1950]

First trade edition. The text is identical to the 1947 edition, but two notes are appended.

642 IONA AND PETER OPIE. The Oxford Dictionary of Nursery Rhymes. *Oxford: At the Clarendon Press.* 1951

For this volume, which treats with the individual histories of 550 rhymes and songs, an attempt was made to assemble everything that had been written on nursery rhymes, to check each quotation with its original source, to survey the contemporary state of oral tradition, and to organise the findings so that any detail would be readily accessible, yet an overall picture emerge. The editors were disconcerted to find themselves spending seven years on what seemed a minor subject. Their reward is that the volume is now in its ninth printing.

8 Transformations and Translations

In each of these rhyme books something has been done to the traditional texts. In some the editors have been unhappy about the rhymes as they found them, and have sought to improve them; in others they have so liked the English rhymes they have wished to introduce them to a wider audience, and have translated them into other languages: French, Swedish, Russian, Japanese, Hawaiian, and Malay. In yet others they have looked upon the rhymes as a source of sport, and have parodied them; or have set them down in unfamiliar ways either for amusement or to make familiar an unfamiliar form of communication. In others, again, they have adjusted the texts to express a particular viewpoint. In this last class are also some of the publicity booklets in the next section.

643 J. GREEN. Margery Daw. Little Boy Blue. No. 7 in J. Green's Nursery Songs. The Words Written, selected or altered, expressly for this purpose, avoiding all objectionable subjects & expressions; The Music Simplified and Fingered for Very Young Performers. *J. Green, 33, Soho Square.* [c. 1825]

644 HENRY DRURY. Arundines Cami sive Musarum Cantabrigiensium Lusus Canori. Collegit atque Edidit Henricus Drury, A.M. *Cantabrigiæ: Typis Academicis Excusus. Veneunt apud J. et J. J. Deighton, Cantabrigiæ; et J. G. Parker, Londini.* 1841

A collection of rhymes and poems rendered in Latin and Greek. Open at versions of 'Three children sliding on the ice' by Francis Hodgson (1781–1852), provost of Eton, and Richard Porson (1759–1808) the Greek scholar.

645 ORIJINAL NURSERI RIMZ, bein an atemt tw substitut plaful sens for serius nonsens. Bi Alecsander Jon Elis, B.A. *Lundun: Fred Pitman, Cwenz Hed Pasej, Paternoster Ro.* 1848

The rhymes in this collection have never caught on.

646 MOTHER GOOSE IN HIERO-GLYPHICS. *Boston: Frederick A. Brown & Co., 29 Cornhill.* 1849

A facsimile, published in London by Victor Gollancz Limited, 1963, of a book issued when hieroglyphics were more popular than they are today.

647 NURSERY RHYMES WITH COLOURED PICTURES. *T. Nelson & Sons, London & Edinburgh.* [c. 1860]

One of 'Nelson's Oil Colour Picture Books for the Nursery', in which each of the rhymes has been poetically embellished. For instance 'Old Doctor O'Kane was a strange sort of man' may be compared with *ODNR* no. 162 and *The Lore and Language of Schoolchildren*, p. 364.

648 CHARLES HARRISON. Ever and a Day. Tales and Rhymes, with Character Pictures. *London: Dean & Son, Publishers, 160a, Fleet Street, E.C.* [c. 1880]

The rhymes are interpreted with pictures and, sometimes, additional couplets that are definitely unconventional.

649 MOTHER GOOSE ON WHEELS. *Father Tuck's Little Pet Series.* [c. 1900]

A collection of nursery rhymes each of which has been adapted by Clifton Bingham to introduce the riding of a bicycle, e.g.,

Jack and Jill rode up the hill,
To fetch a pail of water,
Jack's cycle slipped, and down he tipped
And Jill's came over after.

The gift of Miss G. Rogers-Tillstone.

650 NURSERY RHYMES FOR FIGHTING TIMES. Written by Elphinstone Thorpe, Author of "Lyrics from Lazyland," &c. Illustrated by G. A. Stevens. *London: Everett & Co., Ltd., 42, Essex Street, Strand, W.C.* [1914].

Nursery rhyme parodies written at the beginning of the First World War.

Higgledy-piggledy, my Black Hun!
She lays mines where the trade-ships run!

651 AUSTRALIAN NURSERY RHYMES. Reprinted from "The Red Page", *The Bulletin*, October 18, 1917. *Mirror Reprint*. Threepence.

A sheet giving the prize-winning entries in a competition. The rhymes were used in Australian kindergarten schools.

652 CHARLES POWELL. The Poets in the Nursery. With an Introduction by John Drinkwater. *London: John Lane, The Bodley Head. New York: John Lane Company.* 1920.

A collection of well-known nursery rhymes re-written in the manner of Tennyson, Kipling, Hardy, and other poets.

653 ELIZA GUTCH. L'Entente Cordiale des Bébés. A Selection of English Nursery Rimes done into French For English and French Homes. By E. Gutch, Holgate Lodge, York. *London: T. Werner Laurie, Limited, 30 New Bridge Street, E.C.4.* [1922].

First illustrated edition. The book was originally published the previous year by Herbert Russell in a school edition.

654 A. W. HAMILTON. Malayan Nursery Rhymes. Illustrations by W. G. Stirling. *Printed at The Methodist Publishing House, Singapore.* [1923]

Fifty English nursery rhymes translated into Malay. They had first appeared in a pamphlet the previous year, at the time of the Malaya-Borneo Exhibition. This copy belonged to H. A. Courtney, who did the cover design, and it contains numerous MS. amendments by the translator. The gift of Mr H. W. Pratley.

655 A. W. HAMILTON. Haji's Book of Malayan Nursery Rhymes. Illustrated by Nora Hamerton. Music by H. A. Courtney. *Printers Limited, Singapore.* 1939

A much enlarged edition containing a hundred rhymes in both English and Malay. Presentation copy from 'Haji' (A. W. Hamilton).

656 A. W. HAMILTON. Haji's Book of Malayan Nursery Rhymes. Illustrated by Nora Hamerton. Music by H. A. Courtney. *The Australasian Publishing Co. Pty. Ltd. Sydney and London.* [1947]

Presentation copy from the translator to his musical collaborator. The gift of Mr H. W. Pratley.

657 A. W. HAMILTON. Haji's Book of Malayan Nursery Rhymes. Buku Haji Pantun Budak. Illustrated by Nora Hamerton. *Donald Moore, Singapore.* [1956]

Paperback edition. A further presentation copy to H. A. Courtney. The gift of Mr H. W. Pratley.

658 SAMUEL MARSHAK. С. Маршак. Дом который построил Джек. Английские стихи и песни для детей. Издательство детской лнтературы: Москва, Ленинград. 1936.

Samuel Marshak's translation of 'The House that Jack Built' and other nursery rhymes. Marshak always maintained that the Russian sense of humour was similar to the English, a belief borne out over the years by the continuous popularity in Russia of his translations of English nursery rhymes and nonsense verse.

659 SAMUEL MARSHAK. С. Маршак. Дом, который построил Джек, из английской поэзии для детей. Издательство «Детская литература» Москва, 1967

A recent edition, with coloured frontispiece. Inscribed presentation copy from the translator's son.

660 SAMUEL MARSHAK. Плывёт, плывёт кораблик, английские детские песенки. Пересказал С. Маршак. Рисунки Вл. Конашевича. Москва 1956.

A larger collection of rhymes translated for Russian children. Marshak has written in the English titles; and beneath the renowned rendering of Humpty Dumpty, Korney Chukovsky has converted the translation into English characters. Inscribed presentation copy. With letters on nursery rhymes from Marshak and Chukovsky.

661 DOROTHY WORSLEY. The First Book of ITMA Rhymes, As Sung by Mrs. Handley's Boy Tommy. Music by Clive Richardson & Tony Lowry. Drawings by Cecil Orr. [*Copyright (1945) by the Victory Music Publishing Company, 36 Soho Square, London, W.1.*]

Nursery rhyme parodies in which the heroes are characters in the wartime radio show ITMA ('It's That Man Again').

662 [GEOFFREY HALL] New Nursery Rhymes for Old. ['*True Aim*,' *27, George St., Manchester 1.* 1949. Price Sixpence]

Twelve-page quarto booklet containing 24 rhymes rewritten to eliminate references to everything unpleasant. 'The Old Woman in the Shoe' becomes:

There was an old woman who lived in a shoe,
She had so many children, and loved them
    all too;
She gave them good broth and pieces of bread,
Then kissed them all soundly and put them to bed.

The illustrations are by J. Settle Boon.

663 GEOFFREY HALL and DAVID APPEL. Happy Mother Goose, Familiar Nursery Rhymes For Today's Child. Original Conception by Geoffrey Hall. Adapted by David Appel. Illustrated by William Dugan. *Triangle Publications, Inc.* [1950]

More than a hundred rhymes are given in which the heroes are allowed adventures, but not to be incommoded by them. Thus Jack and Jill fall down the hill, but Jack does so 'like a clown'.

664 ANNE HOPE. Original Nursery Rhymes with Variations. Illustrated by Flora White and Lorna Steele. *Printed and Published by J. Salmon, Sevenoaks.* 1950

The variations, which are double the length of their prototypes, show the economy with which the traditional rhymes are constructed.

665 E. FACKLER. Nice Manners. Pictures to Color. Nursery Rhymes with Manners Lines. Copyright 1952.

The author, a kindergarten teacher in Plymouth, Ohio, has given the nursery rhymes new endings to inculcate the principles of politeness. On one occasion, however, manners seem to be urged rather than morality.

> Little Tommy Tittlemouse,
> Lived in a little house.
> He caught fishes
> In other men's ditches.
> Said Tommy, 'Please pardon me,
> I have no ditch of my own, you see.

Gift of Mrs Cecily Hancock.

666 ALFRED BRISCO. Nursery-Rhyme Land Folks—In Protest. Illustrated by Brian Fawcett. [1952]

Issued by The National Equine (and smaller animals) Defence League. The nursery rhyme characters deny the traditional stories are correct. Mother Hubbard, for instance, says she always had plenty for her dog. Indeed, to judge from the illustration, she was guilty not of underfeeding but of overfeeding it.

667 JEANNIE M. BOGGIE. Old Rhymes in New Dresses. With illustrations. [1953 ?]

Nursery rhymes adapted to local conditions in Gwelo, Rhodesia, where the booklet was printed and published. Gift of Mrs D. Hills.

668 JACK WERNER, edited by. Small Latin and Less Greek. A Small Book of Lighthearted English-Latin Verse with just a sprinkling of the Attic Salt of Greek, Including Nursery Rhymes, Limericks, Epigrams, Epitaphs—in fact, Rhymes Wise & Unwise Generally. Aptly adorned by Haro. *Dennis Dobson Limited, London SW1.* [1954].

669 MIN SKATTKAMMARE. Del I. Rida, rida ranka. Sjunde upplagan. *Natur och Kultur.* [*Stockholm* 1955]

Seventh edition of a popular collection containing translations of rhymes from a number of countries, including Britain. Open at a translation of the 'Crooked Man'. The gift of Mrs Edgar Osborne.

670 FREDERICK WINSOR AND MARION PARRY. The Space Child's Mother Goose. *Simon and Schuster: New York.* 1948

The 16pp prospectus of this accomplished updating of the traditional rhymes.

671 [KENDALL BANNING] Mother Goose Rhymes. *Frederick Muller Limited: London.* [1959]

In this 'censored' edition of Mother Goose, first published in 1926, occasional words in the traditional rhymes have been blacked out to leave the fancy free.

672 TROY E. TABOR. Mother Goose in Hawaii. Songs and Color from the Islands. Illustrations by Lloyd Sexton. *Charles E. Tuttle Company: Rutland, Vermont & Tokyo, Japan.* [1960]

Thirteen Hawaiian translations of English children's songs. Twelve were made especially for this book. The thirteenth, Three Blind Mice, 'already existed in several translations handed down from missionary days of almost 150 years ago'. The gift of Miss Elisabeth Ball.

673 PAUL DEHN. Quake, Quake, Quake. A Leaden Treasury of English Verse. Drawings by Edward Gorey. *Hamish Hamilton: London.* 1961

'Flight-Sergeant Foster flattened Gloucester' and

'Our bomb from the moon came down too soon' are amongst the wittily depressing readjustments to 'the songs of our former innocence'.

674 KORNEY CHUKOVSKY. Корней Чуков-ский, Сказки. Рисунки Д. Васнецова, А. Каневс-кого, В. Конашевича, В. Сумеева. Москва, 1962.

This volume, published to celebrate the eightieth birthday of Russia's beloved children's author, contains at the end some of Chukovsky's translations of English nursery rhymes. A gift during the author's visit to England, June 1962.

675 MICHIO YOSHITAKE. Nursery Rhymes. Selected with Translation and Comments. *Tokyo: Kaibunsha.* 1962.

Presentation copy from the translator, the Professor of English at Kyushu University, who selected the rhymes, notes, and illustrations from *ODNR* and *ONRB*.

676 majic carpet tw nursery riem land. pictures bie gwyneth mamlok. *Initial Teaching Publishing Co. Ltd., 9 Southampton Place, London W.C.1.* [1964].

A book of nursery rhymes transliterated into Pitmans Initial Teaching Alphabet.

677 LUIS D'ANTIN VAN ROOTEN. Mots D'Heures: Gousses, Rames. The d'Antin Manu-script. Edited and Annotated by Luis d'Antin van Rooten. *Angus and Robertson: London: Sydney.* [1968]

First published in the United States in 1967. The editor inherited, he says, a manuscript collection of antique French poems, which, when read aloud in measured tones, have a strangely familiar sound. The joke is skilfully maintained throughout.

678 ORMONDE DE KAY. Rimes de la Mère Oie. Mother Goose Rhymes rendered into French by Ormonde de Kay, Jr. Designed and Illustrated by Seymour Chwast, Milton Glaser, Barry Zaid, of Push Pin Studios. *Little, Brown and Company: Boston, Toronto.* [1971]

Sixty elegant translations, published with lavish illustrations in a book nearly 14 inches tall.

9 Nursery Rhymes in Advertising

Most of the booklets in this section were issued free by manufacturers to enhance the image, or anyway the

sale, of their products. These publications are neces-sarily modest in size; but their quality is usually as good as that of the commercial publications, and several of them contain specially-commissioned work by well-known illustrators. All items, unless otherwise stated, have been lent by Mr Robert Opie from his collection of retail packaging and promotional material.

679 SING A SONG OF SIXPENCE. *London & Otley: William Walker & Sons.* [c. 1860]

An eight-page booklet almost dominated by the fine wood engraving on the back cover advertising Goodall's Household Specialities.

680 CUT-OUT ROCKING SHOWCARD showing little Lord Fauntleroy riding to Banbury Cross hugging a bottle of Mason's Extract of Herbs. [c. 1890]

681 MAYPOLE SOAP MUSICAL NURS-ERY RHYMES. [c. 1890]

682 THE HOUSE THAT KOPS BUILT. Told & Depicted by Wallis Mackay. *Published by Kops Brewery, Wandsworth Bridge Road, Fulham, London.* [1891]

Publicity booklet for a non-alcoholic beer adapt-ing 'The House that Jack Built' to the stages of brewing. The gift of Mr Robert Scott.

683 QUAKER NURSERY RHYMES. Copy-right, 1895, by the American Cereal Co. *Forbes Co. Boston.*

A shaped booklet with puzzle cover containing rhymes whole-heartedly adapted to the promotion of Quaker Oats, e.g.,

> Hi-diddle-diddle!
> Quaker Oats in the middle,
> And a pitcher of cream in plain sight!
> How the little boys laugh!—
> For a dish and a half
> Makes them happy and healthy and bright.

684 OLD MOTHER HUBBARD'S STAR RHYMES. [c. 1895]

A gift booklet issued by Schultz & Co. of New York to promote Star Soap. The nursery rhymes, some of which are German, have not been adapted; but the name 'Star Soap' is worked into each illustration. The gift of Mrs Horatio Hughes.

685 QUEEN OF HEARTS BORWICK'S BAKING POWDER. *Alf Cooke Ltd. Leeds.* [c. 1895]

A folding puzzle which, on the heads-bodies-and-tails principle, makes twelve pictures revealing that the popularity of the queen's tarts was due to their being made with Borwick's Baking Powder.

686 SING A SONG OF SIXPENCE. [*Raphael Tuck & Sons, London, Paris & New York.* c. 1897]

Shaped booklet, overprinted 'Our Christmas Gift', presented to young customers at Frank Wilmer's, Fancy Draper & Milliner, 321 to 329 Mare Street, Hackney.

687 DIAMOND DYE PICTORIAL NURSERY RHYMES. *Forbes Co. Boston.* [c. 1900]

Booklet containing rhymes adapted to the advocacy of Diamond Dyes. The gift of Mrs Horatio Hughes.

688 THIS LITTLE PIG WENT TO MARKET. [c. 1900]

A folder to publicise Cunningham & De Fourier's High Class English Preserved Provisions.

689 RHYMES & TUNES FOR LITTLE FOLKS [1903]; and Part II of Rhymes & Tunes for Little Folks [1904]

Christmas gift booklets issued to promote the products of J. & J. Colman.

690 OUR LITTLE FOLKS NURSERY RHYMES FOR THE VOICE & PIANO. *Published by The People's Music Publishing Compy, 17A Paternoster Row, E.C.* Copyright 1904.

Five of a series of twelve penny music books, each concluding with a nursery song extolling the brands of soap produced by Edward Cook & Co. Ltd, London E.

691 THE SHOP THAT JACK BUILT. [c. 1905]

Gift booklet to publicise Millenium Flour.

692 THE MAGIC PIPER. To the Edinburgh Exhibition by The L. & N. W. & Caledonian Rys. By John Hassall. 1908

A booklet 'showing how & why the Tinker, Tailor, Soldier, Sailor, Richman, Poorman, Apothecary, Thief, went to see the Exhibition'.

693 NURSERY RHYMES AND OTHER POPULAR TALES in relation to Insurance Against Accidents of All Kinds. *Railway Passengers Assurance Co., 64 Cornhill, London.* [c. 1910]

If Cock Robin 'had been prudent enough to take out an ordinary Policy in the Railway Passengers Assurance Company, His Heirs, Executors or Assigns would have been entitled to the full compensation of £1000—in a case of murder of this kind'.

694 NESTLÉ'S PAINTING BOOK, *Eyre & Spottiswoode, H.M. Printers, London.* [c. 1910]

Booklet containing twenty-four postcards, twelve coloured, and twelve plain to be coloured, each with a picture of a nursery rhyme by John Hassall. The gift of Miss Joan Hassall.

695 A NOVELTY FOR THE NURSERY, FROM SHREDDED WHEAT. [c. 1910]

A beautifully worked-out parody of 'The Three Jovial Huntsmen', having a Shredded Wheat biscuit as the *objet trouvé*. Illustrated by John Hassall. This is the artist's copy which he has inscribed 'RARE'. The gift of Miss Joan Hassall.

696 JOHNSTON'S CORN FLOUR IS THE BEST. [c. 1910]

Picture gift cards, 'Old English Nursery Rhymes', promoting corn flour and nursery starch.

697 THE SAUC(E)Y RHYMES PAINTING BOOK. Mary had a little Lamb with lots of H.P. Sauce. [1921]

Coloured illustrations by Lilian A. Govey on alternate pages, with an outline illustration opposite for painting and entering in a competition. Each nursery rhyme is adapted to commend the manufacturer's product.

698 GOLDEN FLEECE MARGARINE. Picture poster by John Hassall. [c. 1925]

Little Jack Horner sat in a corner,
The happiest boy ever seen;
He hadn't a pie—but he'd got on the sly,
Some nice Golden Fleece Margarine.

699 GOLDEN FLEECE MARGARINE Picture poster. [c. 1925]

> Jack Sprat could eat no fat,
> His wife could eat no lean,
> But with the aid of Golden Fleece
> They left the platters clean.

700 THE BOVRIL BOOK OF NURSERY RHYMES. [c. 1939]

In these rhymes the health of nursery rhyme characters is attributed to Bovril. The illustrations are by Madge Williams.

701 POTATO PETE'S NURSERY RHYMES [c. 1944]

Ministry of Food wartime leaflet, with nursery rhyme characters patriotically eating potatoes instead of curds and whey, tarts, and Christmas pie.

702 IZAL NURSERY RHYME PICTURE CARDS. [1937]

Set of 18 cards given with Izal disinfectant and toilet paper. The nursery rhyme on each card has been rewritten.
> Old Mother Hubbard went to the cupboard—
> Her flea-bitten doggie went too;
> Not a bone found they there, but they didn't care,
> They were after the IZAL Shampoo.

703 'A NURSERY RHYME CALENDAR from Cheyney & Sons Ltd.' 1959

A wall calendar designed by Claud Wyatt, with drawings by Margot Gilbert, printed and given away by the Banbury firm of printers who have been active since 1767, and at one time produced chapbooks and other publications for the young.

704 THE COW JUMPED OVER THE MOON. Kellogg's Book of Animal Rhymes. [1961]

Booklet given by Kellogg Company of Great Britain Ltd. in 9 oz. packets of Sugar Ricicles.

705 NOVELTY CARD given to motorists with the compliments of National petrol. Produced by John Catt Ltd. 1963

The turning of a card disc brings an appropriate, or inappropriate, word into a picture window, to complete the rhyme of Miss Muffet. On the back of the card, no matter how the discs are turned, Father's motoring needs are always filled by National products.

706 HEINZ BABY FOODS NURSERY FAVOURITES. *Audio Plastics Ltd.* [1965]

A 45 rpm record issued with the compliments of H. J. Heinz Company Ltd., with the texts of the rhymes on the sleeve.

707 THE NURSERY RHYMES COOKBOOK. Illustrated by Frank Francis. *Published by Spectator Publications Limited for the Dairy Industry.* [1971]

A collection of nursery rhymes each of which is accompanied by an appropriate recipe, such as junket for Miss Muffet, plum cake for the Lion and Unicorn, and bread-and-butter pudding for Tommy Tucker. The book was offered for 65p if two extra 'pintas' were ordered.

10 Nursery Rhyme Novelties

The nursery rhyme is here incidental to the commodity, a mere decoration or gimmick. The oldest novelties are probably the nursery rhyme handkerchiefs, some dating from the 1860s; while others of the handkerchiefs are more recent. Printed cotton nursery rhyme handkerchiefs continue to this day to be a stock-line at Woolworth's. Some nursery rhyme pantomimes are older—if pantomimes count as novelties: the earliest playbill or poster shown here being the one for Harlequin Horner, Or, the Christmas Pie, performed at the Theatre Royal, Drury-Lane, 21 January 1817. The zoetrope bands date from the 'seventies. (The zoetrope itself was produced commercially in 1860.) The nursery rhyme matchbox labels, a set of sixty for 'Nursery Land Safety Matches', belong to the turn of the century; so does the set of playing cards 'Merry Matches: A Capital Round Game for Children', in which the Old Maid is 'Mistress Mary' (Mary Contrary). By this time nursery rhyme playthings were abundant: there were nursery rhyme dolls, nursery rhyme models, nursery

rhyme fancy dresses, and nursery rhyme jigsaw puzzles. We show a fine pair of nursery rhyme jigsaw puzzles, each two-sided, reproducing the plates in Nister's One Two Buckle My Shoe, c. 1901 (no. 146). Since then nursery rhymes have decorated (or disfigured) every kind of juvenile article imaginable. There have been, and still are, nursery rhyme calendars, nursery rhyme notepaper, nursery rhyme postcards, nursery rhyme greeting cards (Margaret Tarrant designed a nice set), nursery rhyme biscuits, nursery rhyme biscuit tins (Caldecott's pictures appear on one of them), and nursery rhyme chocolates. A child can have nursery rhymes on his paper napkins, on his bibs, on his eating utensils, and on his nursery furniture. He can have nursery rhyme Minton tiles, nursery rhyme wallpaper, and complete his décor with plastic nursery rhyme wall plaques. There have long been nursery rhyme tea sets (one with John Hassall's designs), and nursery rhyme mugs: a Little Boy Blue mug has a horn-shaped handle which may be blown; a Sing a Song of Sixpence mug has a bird perched on the handle which whistles. Inevitably there is a piecrust funnel shaped as a blackbird; and a manufacturer who produces Little Miss Muffet Essence of Rennet for making junkets. But we have never understood for whom the Old Woman in a Shoe ashtray was designed, in which the cigarette smoke passes through the old woman's chimney. Is it for nicotine-addicted nippers or for retired nostalgic nannies?

Poetry for Children

A display of first or early appearances of poems written for children has the advantage over a display of adult verse, that it does not consist wholly of poetry books. Some of the best verse for children first appeared embedded in prose; and in this section we find ourselves looking at Goody Two-Shoes, The Water-Babies, Alice in Wonderland, *and* The Wind in the Willows. *Other verses made their bow in periodicals; and no excuse is needed for including here* The Lilliputian Magazine, *1751–52, and the first number of* Good Words for the Young, *1868, and volumes of* Aunt Judy's Magazine. *For the most part, in this section, we confine ourselves to highlights. Little attempt has been made to trace a poem's subsequent fortunes. It would be fascinating to lay side by side twenty or more editions of* Divine Songs *from our holding of Watts, or a like number of parodies and imitations of* Struwwelpeter, *for such a display would convince, as in no other way, the place these works have had in the reading hours of the nation. But these editions would form almost an exhibition in themselves. So we have contented ourselves with giving some subsequent*

popular printings of only two poems: Ann Taylor's My Mother *and William Roscoe's* The Butterfly's Ball, *two titles which became part of the chapbook series, and were commonly published anonymously along with the nursery rhymes.*

708 [JOHN BUNYAN] A Book for Boys and Girls: or, Country Rhimes for Children. By J. B. *London, Printed for N. P. and Sold by the Booksellers in London 1686*

A facsimile of the first edition, of which only two copies are known. Bunyan, in this book, was the first to write verse for children about homely childish subjects, and did so deliberately:

> I would them entice,
> To mount their Thoughts from what are
> childish Toys,
> To Heav'n, for that's prepar'd for Girls
> and Boys.

Oxford Book of Children's Verse, nos. 32–37.

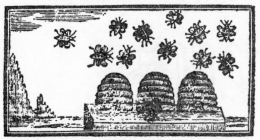

709 JOHN BUNYAN. Divine Emblems: or Temporal Things Spiritualiz'd. Fitted For the Use of Boys and Girls. Adorned with Cuts suitable to every Subject. The Tenth Edition. *London: Printed in the Year 1770. Sold by J. Wilkie, Bookseller, in St. paul's Church-Yard, and M. Booth, at Norwich.*

Numerous editions of Bunyan's Book for Boys and Girls appeared in the eighteenth century but re-titled, as here, *Divine Emblems*.

710 JOHN BUNYAN. Divine Emblems . . . *London. Engraved, Printed and Sold by T. Bennett, No. 7, Plough Court, Fetter Lane Holborn.* [c. 1790]

An edition in which the entire text and illustrations are engraved on copper plates.

711 ISAAC WATTS. Divine Songs Attempted in Easy Language for the Use of Children. *London: Printed for M. Lawrence at the Angel in the Poultry.* 1715

Facsimile, with introduction and bibliography by J. H. P. Pafford, 1971, of the earliest book to contain verses written for the young that are still quoted today.

712 ISAAC WATTS. Divine Songs Attempted in easy Language, for the Use of Children. The Thirteenth Edition. *London: Printed for Richard Ford, at the Angel in the Poultry, over against the Compter.* 1735

The volume is open at the 'Cradle Hymn', which did not appear in the first edition.

Oxford Book of Children's Verse, no. 49.

713 ISAAC WATTS. Divine Songs Attempted in Easy Language, For the Use of Children. The Twenty-First Edition. With some additional Composures. *London: Printed for T. Longman, and J. Buckland, Pater-noster Row* [and others]. 1752

This edition contains 'additional Composures' introduced in the 16th edition.

Mr.ᵗ 9ᵗʰ 1780

Publish'd as ye Act directs by H. Turpin.

714 ISAAC WATTS. Divine Songs . . . To which are added, Supplementary Poems. By Dr. Doddridge. A New Edition. Revised, corrected and enlarged, with Notes, moral and entertaining, and adorned with Copper Plates. *London: Printed for H. Turpin, No. 104, St. John's-street, West-Smithfield.* 1784

Apparently the earliest illustrated edition. Hitherto unrecorded. The first plate is inscribed 'Marh 9th 1780 Publish'd as ye Act directs by H. Turpin'.

715 [G. NESBIT] A Choice Collection of Divine Hymns, & Poems, for Spiritual Instruction and Comfort. 1727.

An example of parental devotion two and a half centuries ago. A manuscript book of 187 closely written pages, wholly in verse, except for the preparatory letter, written for the benefit of an elder daughter, and subsequently copied out for a younger daughter:

For Words more wise, my Care could no where find,
Fit, both to please, and to instruct your mind.

716 [THOMAS FOXTON]. Moral Songs Composed for the Use of Children. *London, Printed for Richard Ford, at the Angel in the Poultry, near Stocks-Market.* 1728.

The first successful work to be inspired by Watts's *Divine Songs;* and one for which the publisher showed good business sense by first obtaining a recommendation from Watts himself.

Oxford Book of Children's Verse, nos. 52–53.

717 [WATTS and FOXTON]. A Choice Collection of Hymns, and Moral Songs; Adapted to the Capacities of Young People, on the several Duties and Incidents of Life. Adorned with elegant Wood-Cuts, to impress more lasting Ideas of each Subject upon the Mind, than can be attained by those in common Use. To which is added, Specimens of Divine Poetry. By several Authors. *Newcastle: Printed by and for T. Saint; and Sold by W. Charnley; and J. Whitfield.* 1781.

In this attractive edition Foxton's poems have been carefully revised, and a number of the cuts are undoubtedly by T. Bewick.

718 [HENRY DIXON] The English Instructor, or, The Art of Spelling Improved. Being a more Plain, Easy, and Regular Method of Teaching Young Children, than any Extant . . . Drawn up for the Use of Schools. *London: Printed for J. Hazard at the Bible near Stationers-Hall, and J. Leake Bookseller at Bath.* 1728

One of two known copies of the first edition of a work that was to be reprinted at least sixty-eight times. 'The Description of a Good Boy', written in words of one syllable, also appeared in many subsequent spelling books.

Oxford Book of Children's Verse, no. 51.

719 'EXODUS CHAP. XX'. Sampler, worked by Mary Vining, begun 22 September 1731, and finished 21 September 1732, embodying The Ten Commandments in verse.

See *Oxford Book of Children's Verse*, no. 54.

720 [NATHANIEL COTTON]. Visions in Verse, for the Entertainment and Instruction of Younger Minds. *London: Printed for R. Dodsley in Pall-mall; And Sold by M. Cooper, at the Globe in Pater-noster-row.* 1751

Cotton was a man who genuinely felt that writing for children was a worthwhile activity:

> Childhood and Youth engage my Pen
> 'Tis Labour lost to talk to Men.

His *Visions*, written in the measure of Gay's *Fables*, are not light-weight in subject-matter, but are gentle in tone; and, happily, were much esteemed when they appeared.

Oxford Book of Children's Verse, nos. 61–62.

721 THE LILLIPUTIAN MAGAZINE: or the Young Gentleman & Lady's Golden Library: being An Attempt to Mend the World, to render the Society of Man More Amiable, & to establish the Plainness, Simplicity, Virtue & Wisdom of the Golden Age, so much Celebrated by the Poets and Historians. *London. Printed for the Society, and Published by T. Carnan at Mr. Newbery's, The Bible and Sun in St. Paul's Church Yard.* [1752]

One of two recorded copies of the first periodical for children. It is now known that a contributor was Christopher Smart, and in particular that he was the author of the lovely 'Morning Hymn' which appeared in the second number, issued June 1751.

Oxford Book of Children's Verse, nos. 65–66.

722 CHARLES WESLEY. Hymns for Children. *Bristol: Printed by E. Farley, in Small-Street.* 1763

Amongst 'Hymns for the Youngest' is 'Gentle Jesus, meek and mild'.

Oxford Book of Children's Verse, no. 56.

723 THE HISTORY OF LITTLE GOODY TWO-SHOES; Otherwise called, Mrs. Margery Two-Shoes. With The Means by which she acquired her Learning and Wisdom, and in consequence thereof her Estate . . . A New Edition, Corrected. *London: Printed for J. Newbery, at the Bible and Sun in St. Paul's Church-yard*, 1766

One of two known copies, the other being in America, of the enlarged second edition of what was undoubtedly the most renowned work of fiction written for young children in the eighteenth century. The well-known 'Epitaph on a Dormouse' comes in part II, chapter IV.

Oxford Book of Children's Verse, no. 74.

724 [CHRISTOPHER SMART] Hymns for the Amusement of Children. Embellished with Cuts. *London. Printed for T. Carnan, in St. Paul's Church Yard.* 1771

This is the only copy in Britain of the first edition of these hymns, which were published anonymously while Smart was in prison for debt. A third edition, 1775, is in the Bodleian, and a Dublin edition, 1772, in the British Museum. An edition for American children was published in Philadelphia, 1791. The original of the frontispiece, a portrait by Benjamin West of the six-year-old Prince Frederick (who was later to be renowned as the 'Brave old Duke of York who had ten thousand men'), is at Buckingham Palace.

Oxford Book of Children's Verse, nos. 67–70; *ODNR*, no. 550.

725 [JOHN HUDDLESTONE WYNNE]. Choice Emblems, Natural, Historical, Fabulous, Moral and Divine, for the improvement and pastime of Youth . . . *London: Printed for George Riley, in Curzon Street, May Fair.* 1772

The first of the nine editions published in the eighteenth century.

Oxford Book of Children's Verse, no. 75.

726 [DOROTHY KILNER] Poems on Various Subjects, for the Amusement of Youth. *London, Printed and Sold by John Marshall and Co. No. 4, Aldermary Church Yard, Bow Lane, London.* [c. 1783]

Ten of the poems are signed M. P., the initials habitually used by Dorothy Kilner; and since the Preface speaks of a single author, and the unsigned poems are not unlike those that are signed, it may be presumed that she was responsible for the whole book, although her sister-in-law, Mary Kilner, may have helped.

Oxford Book of Children's Verse, no. 81.

727 A POETICAL DESCRIPTION OF SONG BIRDS: Interspersed with Entertaining Songs, Fables, and Tales, Adapted to each Subject, for the Amusement of Children. *London: Printed for T. Carnan, at Number 65, in St Paul's Church-yard.* 1787

First published 1773. This is the only copy, of any edition, recorded by Roscoe as being in Britain. The author is unknown, though his name, if discovered, may prove to be one that is well known. His verse on occasion reached a purity—as may be seen—not ordinarily associated with writing for the young.

Oxford Book of Children's Verse, nos. 79–80.

728 WILLIAM BLAKE. Songs of Innocence and Experience Shewing the Two Contrary States of the Human Soul. 1789, 1794. *The Author & Printer W Blake.*

A colour facsimile published by Rupert Hart-Davis Ltd, London, in association with The Trianon Press, Paris, with introduction and commentary by Sir Geoffrey Keynes, 1967.

Oxford Book of Children's Verse, nos. 83–89.

729 LUCY AIKIN. Poetry for Children. Consisting of Short Pieces, to be Committed to Memory. Selected By Lucy Aikin. *London: Printed for R. Phillips, no. 71, St. Paul's; and Sold by B. Tabart, no. 157, New-Bond-Street.* 1801

This was not only an excellent anthology, but the twenty-year-old editor herself contributed some notable pieces.

Oxford Book of Children's Verse, nos. 99–100.

730 [CHARLOTTE SMITH] Conversations introducing Poetry. Chiefly on Subjects of Natural History, for the Use of Young Persons. Volume the First. [Volume the Second.] *London, Printed for John Sharpe, Juvenile Library, London Museum, Piccadilly.* 1815

First published 1804. The Juvenile Library and London Museum was on the other side of Piccadilly to Albemarle Street.

731 [ANN AND JANE TAYLOR, AND OTHERS] Original Poems, for Infant Minds. By Several Young Persons. *London: Printed and Sold by Darton and Harvey, Gracechurch-Street,* 1804

The most popular, as also the most influential collection of children's verse in the nineteenth century, containing, for instance, Ann's poem 'My Mother' which was to be a sentimental bond between parents and children for the next sixty or seventy years. In the Festival of Britain book catalogue it was said the first edition, as shown here, 'must be one of the scarcest books in English literature'.

Oxford Book of Children's Verse, nos. 105 and 110.

732 [ANN AND JANE TAYLOR, AND OTHERS] Original Poems, for Infant Minds, by Several Young Persons. Vol. II. Second Edition, with Additions. *London: Printed for Darton and Harvey, Gracechurch-Street; Sold also by T. Conder, Bucklersbury.* 1806

Published in 1805 following the unexpected success of the first volume.

Oxford Book of Children's Verse, nos. 106–108 and 111.

733 [ANN TAYLOR] My Mother, a favourite Song as Sung at the Public & Private Concerts, taken from Original Poems for Infant Minds. Published by Permission. The Music by J. Dale. *London: Printed for Joseph Dale & Son, Piano Forte Makers (by appointment) to His Royal Highness the Prince of Wales, & Music Sellers to the Royal Family, No 19, Cornhill, the corner of Holles Street, Oxford Street, & No 151, New Bond Street.* [c. 1810]

734 [ANN TAYLOR] Filial Remembrancer. Selection of the Much-Admired Poems, My Father, My Mother, My Brother, and My Sister; with The Father's Address to his Children; in Imitation of Cowper. The Third Edition. *Banbury: Printed and Sold by J. G. Rusher: Sold also by W. Rusher and Son, Banbury: J. Rusher, Reading; and by A. K. Newman & Co., Simkin & Marshall, Evans & Son, Walker & Co., and Law & Whitaker, London; and most other Booksellers.* [c. 1820]

735 [ANN TAYLOR] My Mother. [Dunfermline, *Published by J. Miller & Son*] Price One Halfpenny. [c. 1835]

Printed on yellow paper. Contains also 'My Father'.

736 [ANN TAYLOR] My Mother. *London: Printed for the Booksellers.* [c. 1840]

Chapbook, with publisher's hand-coloured illustrations on four of the eight pages.

737 [ANN TAYLOR] Of A Mother's Care. Rosewarne's New Series of Children's Books, in the most Simple Language the Infant Mind is capable of receiving . . . *Belper: Printed and Sold by J. Rosewarne.* [c. 1840]

The recitation of 'My Mother' takes four of the chapbook's eight pages. The cuts appear to have been executed about 1820.

738 [ANN TAYLOR] My Mother. By Comus, Author of "Three Little Kittens," "Mister Fox," &c. [R. M. Ballantyne]. *London: Thomas Nelson and Sons, Paternoster Row; Edinburgh; and New York.* 1857

Ballantyne sees 'My Mother' as a mother cat, and enlarges on the poem accordingly, in prose and illustration.

739 [ANN TAYLOR] My Mother. *George Routledge and Sons.* [c. 1869]

Routledge's Shilling Toy Books, no. 44.

740 [ANN TAYLOR] My Mother. Walter Crane's Toy Books New Series. *George Routledge & Sons.* [1873]

No. 103 in Routledge's New Sixpenny Toy Books.

741 [ANN TAYLOR] My Mother. *Routledge* [c. 1895]

A paper booklet with coloured illustrations.

742 [ANN and JANE TAYLOR] Rhymes for the Nursery. By the Authors of 'Original Poems'. *London: Printed and sold by Darton & Harvey, Gracechurch-Street.* 1806

Notable for the first appearance of Jane's 'Twinkle, twinkle, little star'. The copy lacks four leaves.

Oxford Book of Children's Verse, nos. 109, 112–114. *ODNR*, no. 489.

743 [ANN and JANE TAYLOR] Select Rhymes for the Nursery, with Copper-plate Engravings. *London: Printed for Darton, Harvey, and Darton, 55, Gracechurch-Street.* 1819

An illustrated selection, first published in 1808, of poems from *Rhymes for the Nursery*.

744 [ANN and JANE TAYLOR] Select Rhymes for The Nursery, With Copper-plate Engravings. *London: Printed for Harvey and Darton, 55, Gracechurch-Street.* 1827. Price One Shilling.

The plates have been re-engraved in this edition.

745 [ANN TAYLOR] The Little Baby's Dance. To Miss Dempster. Little Songs for Little Singers No. 10. By J. Green. *J. Green, 33, Soho Square.* [c. 1825]

Sheet music with pictorial lithographed cover.

746 [JANE TAYLOR] The Little Star; To Miss Julia Barclay & her Brother George, by J. Green. Little Songs for Little Singers No. 4. Second Edition. *John Green, 33, Soho Square.* [c. 1830]

Sheet music with pictorial lithographed cover.

747 [WILLIAM ROSCOE] The Butterfly's Ball, and the Grasshopper's Feast. *London: Printed for J. Harris, corner of St Paul's Church Yard.* Jany 1st 1807.

The engravings are after drawings by William Mulready.

Oxford Book of Children's Verse, no. 121.

748 WILLIAM ROSCOE. The Butterfly's Ball, and the Grasshopper's Feast. By Mr. Roscoe. To which is added, An Original Poem, entitled A Winter's Day. By Mr. Smith, of Stand. *London: Printed for J. Harris and Son, Corner of St. Paul' Church-Yard.* 1819

The cover picture shows Harris's Juvenile Library with St. Paul's in the background.

749 [WILLIAM ROSCOE.] The Butterfly's Ball. *W. Walker & Sons, Otley.* [c. 1860]

A single sheet, 5 × 15 ins., folded to make eight pages. Evidence of the poem's continuing popularity; one of a series that includes Mother Hubbard and The House that Jack Built.

750 [WILLIAM ROSCOE] The Butterfly's Ball and the Grass-hopper's Feast. *T. Nelson & Sons, London & Edinburgh.* [1864 ?]

One of the Nelson's Coloured Picture Books for Children. 'With Elegant Bronze Covers.' Price 6d.

751 [WILLIAM ROSCOE] The Butterfly's Ball. *Otley: William Walker and Sons.* [c. 1865]

'Coloured' edition.

752 [WILLIAM ROSCOE] Panorama of The Butterfly's Ball. *W. Walker & Sons, Otley.* [c. 1870]

A rewritten version. Opens out to 5½ feet.

753 [WILLIAM ROSCOE] The Butterfly's Ball. London & Otley. *William Walker & Sons.* [c. 1890]

A popular edition produced more than eighty years after the poem's first appearance.

754 [WILLIAM ROSCOE] The Butterfly's Ball and the Grasshopper's Feast. Illustrated by Enid Marx. [Bantam Picture Book No. 38. *Transatlantic Arts Ltd., 45 Gt. Russell St., W.C.1.* Price 4d. 1945]

755 [CATHERINE ANN DORSET]. The Peacock "At Home:" A Sequel to the Butterfly's Ball. Written by a Lady. And Illustrated with Elegant Engravings. *London: Printed for J. Harris, Successor to E. Newbery, at the Original Juvenile Library, the Corner of St. Paul's Church-yard.* 1807

So popular was *The Peacock "At Home"* and *The Butterfly's Ball* that between them 40,000 copies were sold in their first year. Two copies are shown: one in blue wrappers with coloured illustrations, the other in buff wrappers with plain illustrations.

Oxford Book of Children's Verse, no. 122.

756 MRS. DORSET. The Peacock 'At Home'. Twenty-fourth Edition. And the Butterfly's Ball and the Grasshopper's Feast: By Mr. Roscoe. With Illustrations by Harrison Weir. *London: Grant and Griffith, Corner of St. Paul's Churchyard.* 1854

One of the last editions to be published for children.

757 [ELIZABETH TURNER] The Daisy, or Cautionary Stories in Verse. Adapted to the Ideas of Children from Four to Eight Years Old. Illustrated with Thirty Engravings on Wood. *London: Printed for J. Harris, Successor to E. Newbery, Corner of St. Paul's Church Yard; and Crosby and Co. Stationers' Court.* 1810

First published 1807. A book inspired by the Taylors' *Original Poems for Infant Minds.*
Oxford Book of Children's Verse, no. 123.

758 [CHARLES AND MARY LAMB] The First Book of Poetry. For the Use of Schools. Intended as Reading Lessons for the Younger Classes. By W. F. Mylius . . . With Two Engravings. A New Edition. *London: Printed for M. J. Godwin and Co. At the City Juvenile Library, 41, Skinner-Street, Snow-Hill; and to be had of all Booksellers.* 1820.

First published 1810. Contains, in this edition, twenty-one pieces from the Lambs' *Poetry for Children,* published the previous year. Why *Poetry for Children,* issued by the same publisher, was allowed to go out of print, while this anthology was fostered, is one of the minor mysteries of juvenile publishing.

759 [WILLIAM WORDSWORTH] The Little Maid and The Gentleman; or, We are Seven. Embellished with Engravings. *York: Printed by J. Kendrew, 23, Colliergate.* [c. 1820]

This juvenile chapbook edition of 'We are Seven' may well have pleased Wordsworth if he knew of it. He once remarked, in a letter to Francis Wrangham, that some of his poems had been composed 'not without a hope' that they might gain a place amongst the half-penny ballads and penny histories of the pedlar's pack.
Oxford Book of Children's Verse, no. 96.

760 THE HISTORY OF SIXTEEN WONDERFUL OLD WOMEN, Illustrated by as Many Engravings; Exhibiting their Principal Eccentricities and Amusements. *London: Printed for Harris and Son, Corner of St. Paul's Church-Yard.* 1821

Plates dated May 1820, and first issued in that year. This is the earliest known book of the verses now known as limericks.
Oxford Book of Children's Verse, no. 140; *ODNR,* nos. 300, 378, 493.

761 ANECDOTES AND ADVENTURES OF FIFTEEN GENTLEMEN. Embellished with Fifteen Coloured Engravings. *London: Printed and Sold by E. Marshall, 140, Fleet Street, From Aldermary Church-Yard.* [c. 1823]

Probably first issued in 1821, this rival publication to the *Sixteen Wonderful Old Women* is reputed to have been written by Richard Scrafton Sharpe; and was illustrated almost certainly by Robert Cruikshank. The book is open to show 'There was a sick man of Tobago', the rhyme which Edward Lear acknowledged was the inspiration for the verses in his *Book of Nonsense,* 1846 (q.v.)
Oxford Book of Children's Verse, no. 141; *ODNR,* nos. 61, 269, 433, 507.

762 THE ORIGINAL FIFTEEN GENTLEMEN, Fathers of All Books of Nonsense, Dug up and Reclothed after Lying in the Dust for Forty Years. *Published by Frederick Arnold, 86, Fleet St. London.* [c. 1865]

A re-styled edition, taking advantage of the popularity of Lear's rhymes.

763 DAME WIGGINS OF LEE and her Seven Wonderful Cats. A Humorous Tale Written principally by a Lady of Ninety. Embellished with Sixteen Coloured Engravings. Price One Shilling. 1823. *London: Dean & Munday, Threadneedle Street; and A. K. Newman & Co., The Minerva Press, Leadenhall Street, E.C.*

A reprint of the original edition, with hand-coloured illustrations, issued by Field & Tuer, The Leadenhall Press, 1887.
Oxford Book of Children's Verse, no. 142.

764 DAME WIGGINS and her seven Wonderful Cats. *London: Dean & Son, Juvenile Book Publishers, 11 Ludgate Hill.* [1865]

An edition by the original publisher, using the original blocks, issued more than forty years after first publication.

765 DAME WIGGINS OF LEE and her Seven Wonderful Cats . . . Edited, with additional verses, by John Ruskin, LL.D., . . . and with new illustrations By Kate Greenaway. With twenty-two

woodcuts. *George Allen, Sunnyside, Orpington, Kent.* 1885

Presentation copy inscribed by Kate Greenaway to her nephew Eddie, to whom, incidentally, her *Mother Goose* was dedicated.

766 DAME WIGGINS OF LEE and her Wonderful Cats. *London: Dean & Son, Limited. 160a, Fleet Street, E.C.* [c. 1910]

Dean's Giant Popular Series no. 62.

767 DAME WIGGINS OF LEE. An Old English Rhyme. *Bantam Picture Books. Transatlantic Arts Ltd. London and New York.* [1944]

Booklet, price 4d, with illustrations similar to those in the original edition.

768 MARY HOWITT. Sketches of Natural History. *London: Effingham Wilson, Royal Exchange.* 1834

Contains 'The Spider and the Fly', and William Howitt's 'The Migration of the Squirrels'. The book is dedicated to two of their children: Alfred, who was to become renowned in Australia as an explorer, and Anna, who was to marry the spiritualist Alaric Alfred Watts.
Oxford Book of Children's Verse, nos. 146 and 150.

769 WILLIAM HOWITT. The Boy's Country-Book: being the Real Life of a Country Boy, written by himself; exhibiting all the amusements, pleasures, and pursuits of children in the country. *London: Longman, Orme, Brown, Green, and Longmans, Paternoster Row.* 1839

This autobiography of childhood, one of the best ever written, contains 'The Wind in a Frolic'.
Oxford Book of Children's Verse, no. 149.

770 MARIA JEWSBURY. The Juvenile Forget-me-not: A Christmas and New Year's Gift, or Birth-day Present. 1833. Edited by Mrs. S. C. Hall. *London: R. Ackermann, 96, Strand; and Westley and Davis, 10, Stationers' Hall Court.* 1833

A fashionable miscellany for the young, which contains the brilliant, though tragic, farewell 'To a Young Brother' by Maria Jewsbury, who, within the year, was to be a victim of cholera in India.
Oxford Book of Children's Verse, no. 154.

771 [SARA COLERIDGE] Pretty Lessons in Verse for Good Children. *London: John W. Parker, West Strand.* 1834

The extremely rare first edition of the book by S. T. Coleridge's talented daughter, which contains the almost proverbial lines
January brings the snow
Makes the feet and fingers glow . . .
written for her three-year-old son Herbert, who was to become the first editor of what is now *The Oxford English Dictionary.*
Oxford Book of Children's Verse, nos. 155–156.

772 WHISTLE-BINKIE; or, the Piper of the Party: being a Collection of Songs, for the Social Circle. Chiefly Original. Edited by Alexander Rodger. Third Series. *Glasgow: David Robertson . . .* 1842

First issued the previous year, when it presented to the world William Miller's 'Willie Winkie'.
Oxford Book of Children's Verse, no. 160; *ODNR*, no. 530.

773 ROBERT BROWNING. The Pied Piper of Hamelin. With 35 Illustrations by Kate Greenaway, Engraved and Printed in Colours by Edmund Evans. *London: George Routledge and Sons, Broadway, Ludgate Hill. Glasgow and New York.* [1888]

Kate Greenaway's depiction of Browning's poem (written in 1842), one of the most aesthetically pleasing of her books.

774 [EDWARD LEAR] A Book of Nonsense. By Derry Down Derry. Part I [Part II].
There was an old Derry down Derry,
Who loved to see little folks merry:
So he made them a Book,
And with laughter they shook,
At the fun of that Derry down Derry!
Published, Feb. 10, 1846, by Thos McLean, 26, Haymarket.

A notorious rarity. Both parts in their original pictorial card covers. These flimsy volumes, consisting simply of lithographed leaves held together at one edge by gutta-percha, mark Lear's entrance into the world of nonsense. Each leaf has a limerick-type verse (he had the idea from 'There was a sick man of Tobago', see item 761); and the 'little folks' who he originally made merry, were the grandchildren of the Earl of Derby at Knowsley Hall, where he was engaged, as an artist, to draw the animals in the Earl's menagerie.
Oxford Book of Children's Verse, no. 164, i–vi.

775 EDWARD LEAR. Nonsense Songs, Stories, Botany, and Alphabets. *London: Robert John Bush, 32, Charing Cross, S.W.* 1871

Contains the first appearance in print of 'The Owl

and the Pussy-Cat', 'The Duck and the Kangaroo', 'The Jumblies', and other classics.
Oxford Book of Children's Verse, nos. 165–9.

776 EDWARD LEAR. More Nonsense, Pictures, Rhymes, Botany, Etc. *London: Robert John Bush, 32, Charing Cross, S.W.* 1872

Contains a further hundred nonsense rhymes, together with nonsense botany, and a nonsense alphabet. The illustration on the cover depicts the famous incident in the railway carriage when Lear (on the right) heard an old gentleman denying that he existed, and produced the name inside his hat and on his umbrella to prove that he did.
Oxford Book of Children's Verse, no. 164, vii–viii.

777 EDWARD LEAR. Laughable Lyrics: A Fourth Book of Nonsense Poems, Songs, Botany, Music, &c. *London: Robert John Bush, 32, Charing Cross, S.W.* 1877

The fifth of the nonsense songs is 'The Pobble who has No Toes'.
Oxford Book of Children's Verse, no. 170.

778 HEINRICH HOFFMANN. The English Struwwelpeter or Pretty Stories and Funny Pictures for Little Children. After the Sixth Edition of the Celebrated German Work of Dr. Heinrich Hoffmann. *Leipsic [sic]: Friedrich Volckmar.* 1848

The first edition of the first English translation of a book that has variously thrilled and dismayed children (not to mention parents) for a hundred and twenty-five years. Less than half a dozen copies of this edition are known to have survived.

779 [CECIL FRANCES ALEXANDER] Hymns for Little Children . . . Seventeenth Edition. *London: Joseph Masters, Aldersgate Street, and New Bond Street.* 1858

First published 1848. This modest little book was remarkable for introducing three of the hymns most sung at children's services, 'All Things Bright and Beautiful', 'Once in Royal David's City', and 'There is a Green Hill'.
Oxford Book of Children's Verse, nos. 171–3.

780 [CECIL FRANCES ALEXANDER] Moral Songs. By the Author of "Hymns for Little Children," Etc. *London: Joseph Masters.* [1849]

Published in the same format as *Hymns for Little Children*, and with similar unpretentious brown cloth covers.
Oxford Book of Children's Verse, nos. 174–5.

781 AUNT EFFIE. Aunt Effie's Rhymes for Little Children. With twenty-four Illustrations by Hablot K. Browne. *London: Addey and Co., 21, Old Bond Street; (late Cundall and Addey.)* [1852]

After much uncertainty and misattribution, it is now established that the author of these popular rhymes was Jane Euphemia Browne (1811–1898), a well-connected lady from Cockermouth, Cumberland, who late in life married The Rev. Stephen H. Saxby, vicar of East Clevedon in Somerset.
Oxford Book of Children's Verse, nos. 191–3.

782 Aunt Effie's Rhymes for Little Children. Set to music by T. Crampton. With Thirty-six Illustrations by Halbot K. Browne. *George Routledge and Sons. London: Broadway, Ludgate Hill. New York: 416 Broome Street.* [1878].

783 MY POETRY BOOK. *London: The Religious Tract Society, 56, Paternoster Row, 65, St. Paul's Church-Yard, and 164, Piccadilly.* [1858]

One of the attractive little anthologies issued by the R.T.S. with colour plates by J. M. Kronheim & Co. It contains the almost traditional 'Table Rules for Little Folks' which governed, or were intended to govern, mealtimes in Victorian homes.
Oxford Book of Children's Verse, no. 196.

784 LULLABIES AND DITTIES FOR LITTLE CHILDREN. *The Religious Tract Society, 56 Paternoster Row; 65 St. Paul's Church-yard; and 164 Piccadilly.* [c. 1870]

Mounted on cloth, with a colour illustration opposite each page of text, which includes 'Table Rules'.

785 [CHARLES HENRY ROSS] Ye Comical Rhymes of Ancient Times, Dug up into Jokes For Small Folks. By C.H.R. *London. Dean and Son, 11 Ludgate Hill, E.C.* [1862]
Oxford Book of Children's Verse, nos. 204–6.

786 CHARLES KINGSLEY. The Water-Babies: A Fairy Tale for a Land-Baby. With Two Illustrations by J. Noel Paton, R.S.A. Second Edition. *London and Cambridge: Macmillan and Co.* 1864.

First published the previous year.
Oxford Book of Children's Verse, nos. 198–200.

787 [WILLIAM BRIGHTY RANDS] Lilliput Levee. With Illustrations by J. E. Millais and G. J. Pinwell. *Alexander Strahan, Publisher, 148 Strand, London.* 1864

Published the year before *Alice in Wonderland* this book provides further confirmation, if such is required, that the standard of children's book production was already high. The lay-out of the title-page, with its illustration by Millais, remains an object lesson to present-day designers.

Oxford Book of Children's Verse, no. 209.

788 [WILLIAM BRIGHTY RANDS] Lilliput Levee. Poems of Childhood, Child-Fancy, and Child-like Moods. *Alexander Strahan, Publisher, 56 Ludgate Hill, London.* 1867

Much of Rand's best verse was not included in the first edition of Lilliput Levee, but in this redesigned edition, with its ornate gilt-blocked cover typical of the period.

Oxford Book of Children's Verse, nos. 210–13.

789 LEWIS CARROLL (Charles Lutwidge Dodgson). Alice's Adventures in Wonderland. With Forty-two Illustrations by John Tenniel. *London: Macmillan and Co.* 1866

First published edition. (Inscription on fly-leaf dated 'Christmas 1865'). Contains, of course, 'You are old, Father William', and the first version of ''Tis the voice of the Lobster: I heard him declare,' the lines that burlesque Watt's poem 'The Sluggard' written one hundred and fifty years before.

Oxford Book of Children's Verse, nos. 218–20.

790 LEWIS CARROLL (Charles Lutwidge Dodgson). A Wreath of Song for Children. Containing The Songs from "Alice in Wonderland," The Songs from "Through the Looking-Glass," and the "Songs for Children," Words by Kingsley, Proctor, MacDonald, Dr. Nield [sic], Herrick, &c., &c. *London: Weekes & Co., 16, Hanover Street, Regent Street, W.* [1872]

Three volumes in one. The music composed by William Boyd. This first musical setting (published separately in 1870) of verses from *Alice* was made with Dodgson's approval, and he supplied two new lines to round off ' 'Tis the voice of the Lobster'.

Oxford Book of Children's Verse, no. 220.

791 LEWIS CARROLL (Charles Lutwidge Dodgson). Through the Looking-Glass, and What Alice Found There. With Fifty Illustrations by John Tenniel. *London: Macmillan and Co.* 1872

Presentation copy from the author, inscription dated 'Christmas 1871'. One of the few sequels to

match up to the original, and in some parts excel it, as in the 'Jabberwocky', 'The Walrus and the Carpenter', 'Humpty Dumpty's Song', and 'The Aged Aged Man'.

Oxford Book of Children's Verse, nos. 221–4.

792 LEWIS CARROLL (Charles Lutwidge Dodgson). Sylvie and Bruno. With Forty-six Illustrations by Harry Furniss. Price Three Half-Crowns. *London: Macmillan and Co. And New York.* 1889

Dodgson's ambitious, or over-ambitious tale, in which as a kind of refrain come verses of the hilarious, or, according to viewpoint, penetratingly philosophic 'Gardener's Song'.

Oxford Book of Children's Verse, no. 225.

793 [MENELLA BUTE SMEDLEY] Aunt Judy's Christmas Volume. For Young People. Illustrated. Edited by Mrs. Alfred Gatty, Author of "Parables from Nature," etc. *London: Bell and Dalby, 186 Fleet Street, and 6 York Street, Covent Garden.* 1866

Gatty family copy (with the bookplate of Alfred Gatty D.D.) of the first volume of this popular magazine. A good start was made in the first number by publishing, along with 'Mrs. Overtheway's Remembrances', Menella Bute Smedley's 'North Pole Story', the heroic poem which was soon to stir the boy Kipling 'to the deeps'.

Oxford Book of Children's Verse, no. 226.

794 [ELIZABETH ANNA HART and MENELLA BUTE SMEDLEY] Poems Written for a Child. By Two Friends. *Strahan and Co., Publishers, 36 Ludgate Hill, London.* 1868

The collection opens with 'A North Pole Story'.

795 [ELIZABETH ANNA HART] Good Words for the Young. Edited by Norman Macleod, D.D. *Strahan & Co, Ludgate Hill, London E.C.* Vol. I, Part 1, November 1, 1868

The first number of the magazine that was to maintain, during its short life, the most consistent excellence of perhaps any children's periodical published before or since. This number, shown here in its original wrappers, contains not only the opening instalment of Kingsley's *Madam How and Lady Why* and George MacDonald's *At the Back of the North Wind*, but the first appearance of Mrs Hart's long-loved poem 'Mother Tabbyskins'.

Oxford Book of Children's Verse, no. 233.

796 JEAN INGLOW. Mopsa the Fairy. Sixth Edition. *London: Wells Gardner, Darton, & Co., 3 Paternoster Buildings, E.C.; And 44 Victoria Street, S.W.*

First published 1869. Contains 'One morning, oh! so early' as part of the story.
Oxford Book of Children's Verse, no. 234.

797 ALFRED SCOTT GATTY. Aunt Judy's Christmas Volume for Young People. Edited by Mrs. Alfred Gatty . . . *London: Bell and Dalby, York Street, Covent Garden.* 1870

Contains Alfred Scott Gatty's 'The Three Little Pigs'.
Oxford Book of Children's Verse, no. 238.

798 ALFRED SCOTT GATTY. The Three Little Pigs, Comic Song, Written and Composed by Alfred Scott Gatty. *London: Robert Cocks & Co., New Burlington St., Regent St., W. By Special Appointment Music Publishers to Her Majesty Queen Victoria & His Royal Highness the Prince of Wales.* [c. 1885]

Music sheet with lithographed pictorial cover.

799 GEORGE MACDONALD. At the Back of the North Wind. *Strahan & Co., Publishers, 56 Ludgate Hill, London.* 1871.

First appearance in book form, following serialisation in *Good Words for the Young*, no. 795. The illustrations are by Arthur Hughes. Contains 'Where did you come from, baby dear? as part of the story.
Oxford Book of Children's Verse, no. 236.

800 JOHN GREENLEAF WHITTIER. Child Life: A Collection of Poems, Edited by John Greenleaf Whittier. With Illustrations. *Boston: James R. Osgood and Company,* 1872

Whittier includes his own poem 'In School-Days'.
Oxford Book of Children's Verse, no. 235.

801 CHRISTINA G. ROSSETTI. Sing-Song. A Nursery Rhyme Book. With One Hundred and Twenty Illustrations by Arthur Hughes. Engraved by the Brothers Dalziel. *London: George Routledge and Sons, The Broadway, Ludgate.* 1872

A book in which the illustrations and layout beautifully match the verses.
Oxford Book of Children's Verse, nos. 240–253.

802 JULIANA HORATIA EWING. Aunt Judy's Christmas Volume for 1873. Edited by Mrs.

Alfred Gatty . . . *London: George Bell and Sons, York Street, Covent Garden.* 1873

Contains Mrs. Ewing's 'The Willow-Man'. The illustration for it is by S. Hall.
Oxford Book of Children's Verse, no. 228.

803 JULIANA HORATIA EWING. The Dolls' Wash. Pictured by R. André. *London: S.P.C.K. New York: E. & J. B. Young & Co.* [1883]

First separate edition. One of sixteen matching volumes reprinting Mrs Ewing's narrative poems.
Oxford Book of Children's Verse, no. 230.

804 SYDNEY DAYRE (MRS COCHRAN). St. Nicholas: An Illustrated Magazine for Girls and Boys, conducted by Mary Mapes Dodge. Volume VIII. Part I., November, 1880, to May, 1881. *New-York: Scribner & Co. (Incorporated 1870).* London: *F. Warne & Co.*

The leading monthly magazine for children in the United States in the latter part of the nineteenth century. Contains, in the April number, 'A Lesson for Mamma' by Sydney Dayre.
Oxford Book of Children's Verse, no. 259.

805 WILLIAM ALLINGHAM. Rhymes for the Young Folk. With Pictures by Helen Allingham, Kate Greenaway, Caroline Paterson, and Harry Furniss. Engraved and Printed by Edmund Evans. *Cassell and Company, Limited, London, Paris, New York and Melbourne.* [1887]

The collected edition of Allingham's verse for children which he had begun writing almost half a century earlier. The introductory drawing by his wife Helen shows Allingham introducing a child to one of the 'wee folk'. Presentation copy, inscribed by Helen Allingham to an aunt and uncle. Shown with two letters from Caldecott about the possibility of his illustrating the volume.
Oxford Book of Children's Verse, nos. 186–9.

806 SEE-SAW; A Book of Songs and Pictures from "St. Nicholas." With Original Music by William M. Hutchinson . . . *London: Frederick Warne and Co., Bedford Street, Strand.* [c. 1890]

This selection includes Mrs Corbett's 'Three Wise Women' and Laura E. Richards' 'Uncle Jehoshaphat'.
Oxford Book of Children's Verse, nos. 257 and 262.

807 [WILLIAM CORY.] Ionica. *George Allen. London and Orpington.* 1891

Second edition; but the first to include 'A Ballad for a Boy'.
Oxford Book of Children's Verse, no. 265.

808 ROBERT LOUIS STEVENSON. A Child's Garden of Verses. *London: Longmans, Green, and Co. 1885.*

The modest, unillustrated, original edition of a book of which a new illustrated edition now appears almost every year. A few examples follow.

Oxford Book of Children's Verse, nos. 266–281.

809 ROBERT LOUIS STEVENSON. A Child's Garland of Songs. Gathered from A Child's Garden of Verses and Set to Music by C. Villiers Stanford. *London: Longmans, Green, & Co., And New York: 15 East 16th Street. 1892.*

A selection, set to music and illustrated, with a special introduction by R.L.S. beginning:

Come, my little children, here are songs
    for you,
Some are short, and some are long, and
    all, all are new.

810 ROBERT LOUIS STEVENSON. A Child's Garden of Verses. Illustrated by Charles Robinson. *London: John Lane, The Bodley Head. New York: Charles Scribner's Sons. 1896.*

First complete illustrated edition.

811 ROBERT LOUIS STEVENSON. A Child's Garden of Verses. With Wood Engravings by Joan Hassall. *Edinburgh: The Hopetoun Press. 1947*

It is difficult to conceive that there will ever be a nicer edition than this, so perfectly do the engravings complement the mood of the verses.

812 ROBERT LOUIS STEVENSON. A Child's Garden of Verses. Translated by Michio Yashitake. *Tokyo. 1955.*

A Japanese edition. Presentation copy from the translator. The illustrations are by the translator's daughter, aged eleven.

813 CHARLES E. CARRYL. St. Nicholas: An Illustrated Magazine for Young Folks Conducted by Mary Mapes Dodge. Volume XIX. Part I., November, 1891, to April, 1892. *The Century Co., New York. T. Fisher Unwin, London.*

'The Camel's Complaint', which comes in Charles E. Carryl's story *The Admiral Caravan,* appeared in the April number.

Oxford Book of Children's Verse, no. 286.

814 HILAIRE BELLOC. The Bad Child's Book of Beasts. Verses by H. B. Pictures by B. T. B. [Lord Basil Blackwood]. *Oxford: Alden & Co. Ltd., Bocardo Press, 35, Corn-Market Street. London: Simpkin, Marshall, Hamilton, Kent and Co. Ltd. [1896]*

Oxford Book of Children's Verse, nos. 292 and 293.

815 HILAIRE BELLOC. More Beasts (for Worse Children). Verses by H. B. Pictures by B. T. B. [Lord Basil Blackwood]. *Published by Edward Arnold, London and New York. [1897]*

Oxford Book of Children's Verse, nos. 294 and 295.

816 HILAIRE BELLOC. Cautionary Tales for Children. Designed for the Admonition of Children between the ages of eight and fourteen years. Verses by H. Belloc. Pictures by B. T. B. [Lord Basil Blackwood]. *London: Eveleigh Nash. [1907]*

Oxford Book of Children's Verse, nos. 296 and 297.

817 EDWARD ABBOTT PARRY. The Scarlet Herring And other Stories. With Illustrations by Athelstan D. Rusden. *London: Smith, Elder, & Co., 15 Waterloo Place. Manchester: Sherratt & Hughes, 27 St. Ann Street. 1899*

'The Jam Fish' appears as part of the story of the Golden Jujube.

Oxford Book of Children's Verse, no. 291.

818 RUDYARD KIPLING. Just So Stories for Little Children. Illustrated by the Author. *London: Macmillan and Co., Limited. 1902*

Oxford Book of Children's Verse, no. 299.

819 RUDYARD KIPLING. Puck of Pook's Hill. *London: Macmillan and Co., Limited. 1906*

The illustrations are by H. R. Millar.

Oxford Book of Children's Verse, nos. 300–301.

820 RUDYARD KIPLING. Rewards and Fairies. With Illustrations by Frank Craig. *Macmillan and Co., Limited, St. Martin's Street, London. 1910*

Oxford Book of Children's Verse, 302–303.

821 WALTER DE LA MARE. Songs of Childhood. With Illustrations by Estella Canziani. New Edition. *Longmans, Green and Co. 39 Paternoster Row, London, E.C.4. New York, Toronto, Bombay, Calcutta and Madras. 1923*

First illustrated edition. The illustrator's copy,

with Miss Canziani's bookplate, and a compliments slip from the publisher tipped in. The book was originally published in 1902 under the pseudonym Walter Ramal.

822 KENNETH GRAHAME. The Wind in the Willows. *New York: Charles Scribner's Sons.* 1908

Inscribed presentation copy, October 1908, from the author to his only child, Alastair, for whom the story was invented. 'Ducks' Ditty' comes in chapter II.
Oxford Book of Children's Verse, no. 311.

823 ELEANOR FARJEON. Nursery Rhymes of London Town. Illustrated by Macdonald Gill. *London: Duckworth & Co., Henrietta Street, Covent Garden, W.C.* [1916]

Advance copy, with publisher's stamp. 'Blackfriars' has already appeared in collections as a traditional nursery rhyme.
Oxford Book of Children's Verse, no. 314.

824 [ROSE FYLEMAN] Punch. Vol. CLII. [*London: Published at the Office, 10, Bouverie Street, E.C.4.*] 1917

Rose Fyleman's 'Fairies' appeared in the number for 23 May, 1917, launching her as a writer for children.
Oxford Book of Children's Verse, no. 319.

825 [ROSE FYLEMAN] Punch. Vol. CLIV. [*London: Published at the Office, 10, Bouverie Street, E.C.4.*] 1918

Rose Fyleman's meteoric rise to popularity is here evident. She has been a contributor to *Punch* for only eight months, and her first book has not yet been published, but she is given the opening page of the new volume, and is allowed to sign the poem with her initials.
Oxford Book of Children's Verse, no. 320.

826 ROSE FYLEMAN. Fairies and Chimneys. *Methuen & Co., Ltd., 36 Essex Street W.C., London.* [2 May 1918.]

The original price was 3s. 6d., which seems high for a 45pp. unillustrated booklet, yet twelve printings were needed in four years.
Oxford Book of Children's Verse, 319–322.

827 A. A. MILNE. Punch Vol. CLXVI. [*London: Published at the Office, 10, Bouverie Street, E.C.4.* January–June 1924]

The first appearance here of more than half the verses that make up *When We Were Very Young* is not of significance in the way that was Punch's publication of Rose Fyleman's verses. A. A. Milne was an established writer, and the book was already printing. In fact he was reluctant to give the editor pre-publication rights in case it affected the book's sale. He need not have worried. In the first two months six printings were required, and forty-nine years later the book still sells strongly.
Oxford Book of Children's Verse, nos. 325–327.

828 A. A. MILNE. When We Were Very Young. With Decorations by Ernest H. Shepard. *Methuen & Co. Ltd. 36 Essex Street, London W.C.* [6 November 1924]

First issue, with the blank endpapers. Extra decorated by Ernest Shepard on the title-page. An unadorned first edition is placed alongside for comparison.
Oxford Book of Children's Verse, nos. 325–328.

829 T. S. ELIOT. Old Possum's Book of Practical Cats. *Faber and Faber Limited, 24 Russell Square, London.* [1939]
Oxford Book of Children's Verse, nos. 330 and 331.

Our songs are done, the voices hushed
That rose so fresh and free.
To sleep now go, and dream in peace;
Even the sweetest songs must cease
When night has sovereignty.

70